Round the World Handbook

Round the World Handbook

Roy Woodcock

Hamlyn
London · New York · Sydney · Toronto

Published 1978 by
The Hamlyn Publishing Group Limited
London . New York . Sydney . Toronto
Astronaut House, Feltham, Middlesex, England
© Copyright The Hamlyn Publishing Group Limited 1978

ISBN 0 600 39530 8

Printed in Italy

Acknowledgements

Illustrations by Gerald Witcomb.
A number of the illustrations in this book originally appeared in Hamlyn all-colour paperbacks, Hamlyn Junior Science Encyclopedia, and Hamlyn My World of Geography.

Photographs
Professor N. N. Ambraseys, Imperial College of Science and Technology, London 35; Aquila Photographics, Studley 113; Australian News Service, London 227, 228; Bowater Corporation, London 111, 140; P. G. Boxhall 199; British Airways 142; British Steel Corporation, London 139; J. Allan Cash, London 131; Bruce Coleman – Gene Ahrensk 119; Bruce Coleman – Jen and Des Bartlett 103; Bruce Coleman – Douglas Botting 211; Bruce Coleman – Gerald Cubitt 130, 213; Bruce Coleman – Nicholas de Vore 232; Bruce Coleman – Francisco Erize 233; Bruce Coleman – Jerry Hout 154; Bruce Coleman – Masud Quraishy 202; Bruce Coleman – Norman Tomalin 80; Serena Fass, London 102, 216, 217; Fiat S.P.A., London 140–141; French Government Tourist Office, London 125; Hamlyn Group Picture Library 27, 60, 189, 195, 231; D. Hodges, London 196; Hoverlloyd, London 165; Leigh Jones, Woking 192, 193, 197; Lipton Ltd., London 105; Massey-Ferguson, London 109; NASA, Washington D.C. 11 top; Picturepoint, London 51; G. R. Roberts, Nelson, New Zealand 93; South African Tourist Corporation, London 207; Tate and Lyle, London 124; Tony Taylor – Birds of Paradise 9, 179; Andy Vargo, Western Turville 41, 54, 57, 95, 157, 161, 170, 171, 172, 173, 174, 175, 176, 177; Varig (Brazilian Airlines), London 182; Vautier–Decool, Paris 158; ZEFA – P. W. Bading 45; ZEFA – D. Baglin 97; ZEFA – K. Biedermann 145; ZEFA – J. Bitsch 181; ZEFA – Werner Braun 55; ZEFA – R. Everts 96; ZEFA – H. Gaertner 169; ZEFA – R. Halin 61, 107; ZEFA – G. Heil 184; ZEFA – Icelandic Photo 138; ZEFA – Hans Kramarz 212; ZEFA – Leidmann, Nagold 209; ZEFA – Mohn 49; ZEFA – W. Ostgathe 190; ZEFA – V. Phillips 149; ZEFA – J. Plaff 143; ZEFA – E. Rekos 186; ZEFA – K. Röhrich 223; ZEFA – D. Schmidt 121; ZEFA – H. Schmied 39; ZEFA – K. Scholz 201; ZEFA – J. Schörken 229; ZEFA – Starfoto 221 bottom; ZEFA – I. Steinhoff 92; ZEFA – D. Wüst 79.

Contents

Introduction

Geography is a very large and fascinating subject, covering the study of landscape – with all the natural phenomena such as hills, plains, rivers, forests and grassland – as well as man-made features such as roads, dams and agricultural developments. The former is known as physical geography and the latter as human geography.

Factual knowledge is an important aspect of this study, though it is clearly impossible for anyone to learn more than a fraction of the subject. Geography is also a visual and practical subject – no matter where you are in the world, you can look at geographical phenomena. For example, it is interesting working out why urban areas have grown up in some locations and not in others, and why some regions contain many inhabitants, but others are empty.

Practical geographical field-work is possible everywhere, and it can be very rewarding. You can study the local geography at home or on holiday by looking at all kinds of geographical features – factories, roads, hills, valleys, forests, the seaside and so on. You will notice many such features at the seaside. There may be cliffs in which rock strata can be seen; beaches showing how rocks are broken up into sediment; and channels in the sand like miniature rivers.

Try your skill at identifying features in the scene shown on the title page. It shows a group of young field-workers at the seaside exploring a very interesting stretch of beach. You may be surprised how many things you will find in the picture.

Geography is a dynamic, ever-changing subject, always offering new and exciting things to think about. What thought first comes into your head when you hear the word 'Viking'? Do you think of the original Vikings – the handsome Norwegians who took to a maritime life and journeyed to new lands? Or does your mind turn to the modern Vikings – the spacecraft which travelled all the way from the earth to Mars?

This book is packed with information on a wide range of geographical subjects, and is designed to provide keen young geographers with an easy and speedy source of reference. The solar system, physical features of land and sea, weather and climate, people, crops and minerals are all featured in the following pages. There is a section dealing with the countries of the world, too, with hundreds of useful facts and figures. And there's an index at the end to enable you to look up information quickly.

Adding special interest to the book are the lists of Things to Do,

Barbados sunset – the red sky at night
forecasting sunshine tomorrow.

which can be found at the end of
several sections. These are practical
suggestions to encourage active
involvement in field-work and
study.

Geography is a living subject,
with new events taking place every
day. Modern man has so many
opportunities of finding out about
the world around him – through

newspapers, books, radio, television
and travel.

Sitting back in an armchair listen-
ing to a radio programme or watch-
ing television, one can be transported to the other side of the world
and be given exciting new insights
into different places, people and cul-
tures.

Geography is present and around
us all the time. Everything we can
see is part of this fascinating subject,
to be enjoyed by people of all ages.

The Solar System

The solar system is spread in a disc shape over 90 000 light years. (Each light year is more than 9 million million kilometres). It includes the planets Mercury, Venus, Earth, Mars, Jupiter, Saturn, Uranus (only discovered in 1781), Neptune (discovered in 1846) and Pluto (1930), in that order of increasing distance from the Sun. The Earth is at an average distance of 150 million kilometres from the Sun, Mars is at 228 million kilometres and Pluto at 5910 million kilometres. The planets move around the Sun at different rates. Pluto takes 248 years to complete its circuit, Neptune 165 years and Mars 687 days.

The first Mariner space craft from the United States of America flew past Mars in 1969, and Viking I went into orbit and sent down a small landing craft in 1976. More is now known about Mars as a result of these recent events, but no evidence of advanced forms of life has been found.

Much more is known about the Moon than Mars. The Moon is not a planet; it is a satellite of the Earth. It is only 380 000 kilometres away from the Earth and travels in orbit around the Earth once every 29

The Solar System. 1. Mercury 2. Venus 3. Earth 4. Mars 5. The Asteroids 6. Jupiter 7. Saturn 8. Uranus 9. Neptune 10. Pluto.

Viking 2 on Mars' Utopian Plain, showing red boulder strewn landscape.

days. As the Moon travels in its orbit, light from the Sun shines on it making it visible from Earth. The size of the moon as we see it varies according to the time of the month. When it lies between Earth and Sun we cannot see it, but as it moves in its orbit, it seems to grow and change shape as the Sun illuminates more and more of it. Then it gets smaller again, and disappears. Thus we see what we call a new Moon, a half Moon, a full Moon and a waning Moon in sequence. These are called the different *phases* of the Moon.

The Earth travels round the Sun in an elliptical orbit every 365¼ days. Each year lasts 365 days, and the quarters add up to make an extra day every fourth year. This is how leap years come about.

As well as revolving around the Sun, the Earth also rotates on its own axis once every 24 hours. Half of the Earth faces the Sun and receives daylight whilst the other half faces away and is in darkness.

A picture of the earth taken from the surface of the moon.

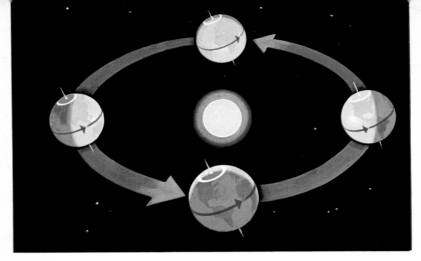

The changing position of the earth, relative to the sun, causes the seasons.

This is why we have day and night. As the Earth spins round from west to east, different parts of the planet receive daylight. On Earth we get the impression that the Sun rises in the east, travels across the sky during the day and sets in the west, but in reality it is not the Sun which is moving, but the Earth. Easterly locations receive daylight first, and their clock time is therefore earlier. For example, Australia receives light 10 to 11 hours before Britain.

The Earth revolves through 360° in 24 hours. Every 15° of longitude (lines of longitude are the north to south lines which run from the North Pole to the South Pole) represent a difference of one hour in time, because of the movement of the Earth on its own axis. This movement causes time differences

each day, whilst the movement of the Earth around the Sun every year causes the seasons. The Earth's axis is tilted at 23½° and therefore in its journey around the Sun, there is a

The earth revolves every 24 hours and receives daylight whilst facing the sun.

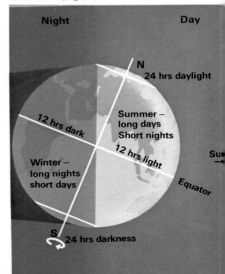

period in June when the northern hemisphere is tilting towards the Sun. This gives rise to the northern summer, while winter is occurring south of the equator. Six months later, the southern hemisphere is tilting towards the Sun, and so experiences summer, whilst winter is in progress north of the equator.

Standard time is normally taken to be the 0° meridian which runs through Greenwich in London. If the time was midday on a Monday in London, the time would be 1300 hours at 15°E or 1100 hours at 15°W. 180°E would be 12 hours ahead of Greenwich, i.e. midnight on Monday, whereas 180°W would be 12 hours behind Greenwich, i.e. midnight on Sunday. But 180°E and 180°W are actually the same line of

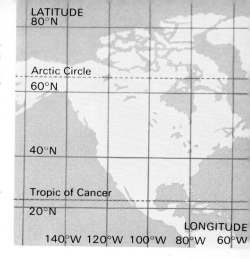

The framework of lines of latitude and longitude.

longitude. We call this imaginary line the *International Date Line*. A person travelling from east to west goes ahead 24 hours upon crossing the line, while a person travelling in an easterly direction goes back 24 hours. The International Date Line diverges from the 180° meridian in a few places such as Fiji and the Aleutian Islands.

Other time problems are solved by having time zones. Large countries endeavour to regulate time and reduce confusion by having set zones with standard times. The U.S.A. has 7 time zones.

Lines of longitude are much wider on the equator than at the N. and S. poles, where they all converge on a point. Lines of latitude on the other hand are all equidistant, about 110 kilometres apart.

The North American Time Zones showing time when midday at Greenwich.

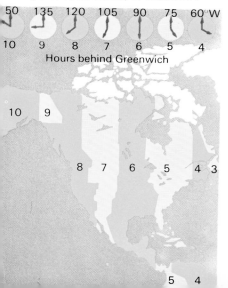

The Structure of of the Earth

The Earth's Crust

The earth has an area of 510 million square kilometres. The earth is not a true sphere; it is an oblate spheroid because there is a slight flattening at the poles and a slight bulge at the equator. The diameter through the equator is 12 744 kilometres while through the poles it is 12 703 kilometres. The circumference around the equator is 40 059 kilometres and round the poles is 39 995 kilometres.

The earth's formation is not fully known or understood but it is thought to have solidified from gaseous matter about 5000 million years ago. As it solidified, one large land mass, which was named 'Pangaea', was created. Later this split into two land masses, known as Gondwanaland and Laurasia, and these subsequently formed the present-day continents.

We can imagine that the earth is like an onion in the way that it consists of layers. The outer layer is called the *crust* (lithosphere) and it is between 5 and 50 kilometres thick. The crust can normally be subdivided into *sial* and *sima*. The sial layer (*si* from silica and *al* from aluminium) consists of sedimentary and granitic rocks, and makes up the continents. The sima (*si* from silica and *ma* from magnesia) is beneath the sial and consists of denser basic rocks. In the oceans the sial is generally thin or non-existent.

Beneath the crust is the *mantle* (mesosphere), which consists of denser basic or ultra-basic rocks. The mantle is separated from the crust by the Mohorovicic discon-

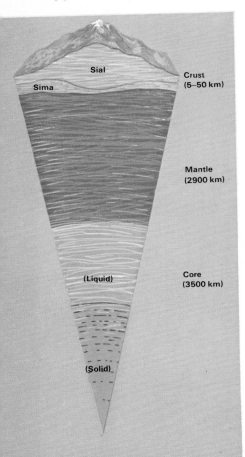

The layers of rock from the outer crust to the centre of the earth.

tinuity, which is a distinct break or change of rock type, first discovered by the Yugoslavian geologist, Mohorovicic. This discontinuity is generally known as the Moho. The mantle is about 2900 kilometres thick and is separated from the core by the Gutenberg discontinuity, another sharp break.

The *core* (barysphere) is probably metallic in character, and this consists of ferro-nickel minerals. Heat increases downwards beneath the surface of the earth and therefore it is very hot. Temperatures are so high that the rocks should melt but it is thought that the pressure from the mantle and crust prevents this from happening. The outer part of the core is liquid or plastic, but the inner core is thought to be solid.

Information about the mantle and core has been collected by the study of earthquake waves, which react differently in rocks of different densities. Knowledge of the interior of the earth is limited, as the deepest penetration by boring is only about 6 kilometres. Information about the earth is also revealed by volcanoes bringing up materials from great depths and throwing them onto the surface. This is why geological research teams are often to be found in dangerous locations near active volcanoes.

The sial is rather like a raft floating on the sima, as there are slow but continuous movements of the surface rocks of the earth. An American called Taylor and an

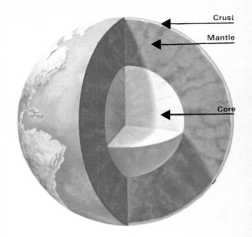

A section through the earth to show the different layers.

Austrian called Wegener both suggested, early in the twentieth century, that the large scale movement of continents may have taken place.

Alfred Wegener published a book, in 1915, on the origins of the oceans and continents, and in it he stated that continents had drifted about in the past. The strongest evidence he had to support this theory was the way in which South America fitted into the Guinea coast region of Africa. He had no real proof however and this theory was ignored until the 1960s.

At that time the studies of palaeomagnetism were just being developed. When molten rocks are thrown up by erupting volcanoes, they contain magnetic particles. As the rocks cool and solidify, the magnetic particles orientate them-

15

selves to point towards the magnetic pole. Any old igneous rocks can now be analysed and their magnetic particles will reveal where the rocks were at the time of formation. Palaeomagnetic studies have shown that Africa, South America and Australia must have been close together in the past, and that they represent the original large land mass which has been named Gondwanaland.

Geologists were also researching the idea that the heat of the earth caused convection currents within the mantle, and there was growing evidence in the 1950s and 1960s to show that this really was so. The convection currents provided the mechanism which enabled the continents to move and radioactive materials within the earth provided the heat to sustain the currents.

Since 1960, geologists have learnt much about the ocean floor. Studies have shown that new rocks are reaching the surface on the beds of some oceans, and spreading out sideways. The ocean floor is actually spreading and new rocks are filling up the crack which is left behind. The spreading of the ocean floor means that the surface of the earth is drifting sideways as suggested by Wegener in 1915. So, the theory of continental drift has now been proved.

Theories about convection currents beneath the earth's crust.

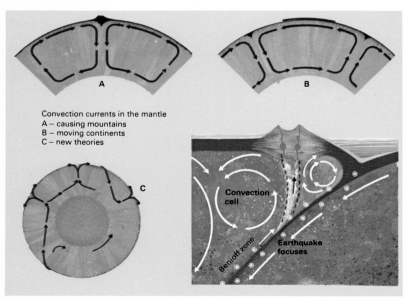

Convection currents in the mantle
A – causing mountains
B – moving continents
C – new theories

Convection cell

Benioff zone

Earthquake focuses

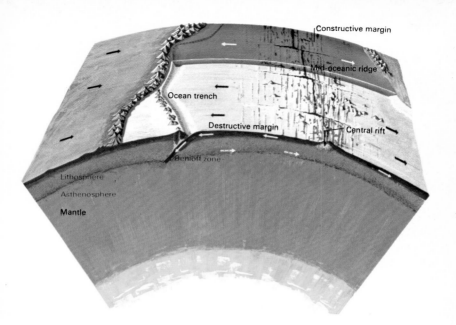

Crustal movements and the formation of trenches and oceanic ridges.

Recent research has shown that the earth's crust consists of a series of plates which fit together like the pieces of a jigsaw puzzle. The plates do not always fit smoothly as the correct pieces of a jigsaw do, and where unevenness occurs there can be very serious earth movements such as earthquakes, volcanoes or orogenesis (which means the formation of mountains). Because of the convection currents, the plates move – sometimes together, sometimes apart – thereby creating the serious earth movements.

Continents

	Area in sq km	Av. elevation in metres
Land surface	148 950 000	
Asia	43 882 000	910
Africa	30 285 000	580
North America	24 255 000	600
South America	17 819 000	550
Antarctica	13 338 000	1830
Europe	10 497 000	300
Australasia	7 687 000	300

Oceans and Large Seas

	Area in sq km	Av. depth in metres
Water surface	361 150 000	
Pacific	165 724 000	4280
Atlantic	82 217 000	4230
Indian	60 476 000	3960
Arctic	14 351 000	1280
Mediterranean	2 965 000	1370
North Sea	572 000	55
Baltic Sea	409 000	70

The Oceans

If the surface of the earth is measured for its height above or below sea level, it can be discovered how much land lies between, say, 100 and 1000 metres above sea level.

A graph can be drawn to show the amount of land between certain levels, and this is called the hypsographic curve. This curve shows that much of the sea bed is 5000 metres below sea level, whereas the commonest height of the land surface is less than 1000 metres. The oceans occupy 70·8% of the total area of the earth, and the land surface occupies 29·2%. The average height of the land is less than 1000 metres but the average depth of the sea is nearly 4000 metres. The total vertical range between the highest point of the land (8742 metres) and the deepest part of the ocean (11 340 metres) is 20 082 metres, or 20 kilometres. This is only a tiny fraction of the earth's diameter – less than one-fifth of one per cent.

From the hypsographic curve you will notice that the extent of high mountains is small and that the continental masses are quite low. The shallow part of the sea is called the *continental shelf* and it is really a continuation of the coastal plain. It is an area covered only by shallow water, to a depth of 100 fathoms. Off some continents it extends quite a long way – in the North Sea area for example – while elsewhere, such as Western South America, it is small. Land sediment usually accumulates in these areas, and the shallow waters often provide good fishing grounds.

The edge of the continental shelf is shown by a slight increase in gradient which is called the *continental slope*. It is normally no steeper than 5° but the hypsographic curve diagram has an exaggerated vertical scale which makes it look much steeper. The continental slope leads down to the deep sea plain, which is broken up by occasional troughs or trenches, or by mountains. These higher parts may be considerable mountain ranges or simply isolated peaks, which are known as *guyots*. The deep ocean floor occupies one-third of the surface of the earth. The ocean deeps are often quite narrow, but are very steep-sided and are vir-

Hypsographic curve showing percentages of the earth's surface at different heights.

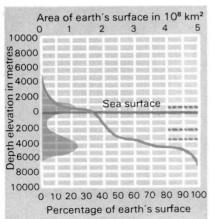

Area of earth's surface in 10⁸ km²

Sea surface

Depth elevation in metres

Percentage of earth's surface

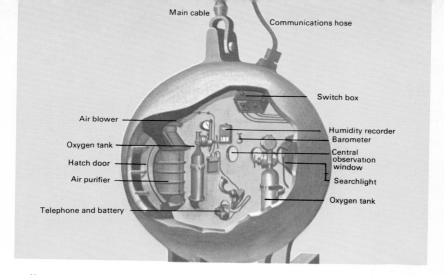

tually unknown, in spite of exploration in bathyspheres (submersible observation chambers).

Barton's bathysphere, which dived to a depth of 923 metres in 1934.

There are four major oceans, or five if the Southern or Antarctic Ocean is regarded as separate. The Pacific is by far the largest. It is widest near the equator and very narrow in the north, where the Bering Straits provide the only link with the Arctic. It is wide in the south where it extends to Antarctica. It is mostly surrounded by high mountains, has little or no continental shelf, and contains many deeps. Volcanic and coral islands stand up from deep sea plains. The Marianas Trench off the island of Guam is the deepest area of water, reaching nearly 10 kilometres.

The Atlantic Ocean is less than half the size of the Pacific and is vaguely S-shaped. The middle of the ocean is followed by a north-south ridge extending from Iceland and associated with much recent volcanic activity. The continental shelf is broad off N.W. Europe, eastern Canada and Patagonia. The deeps are fewer and smaller than in the Pacific, and only reach 8 kilometres at a maximum.

The Indian Ocean is mostly in the Southern Hemisphere and is much more uniform and regular than the Pacific and Atlantic. The only deep trench is the Sunda Trench, to the south of Java.

There is a remarkable lack of knowledge about the oceans because of the difficulties of studying the sea-bed, and even the difficulties of studying sea-water itself. Rough water and oceanic movements have both caused prob-

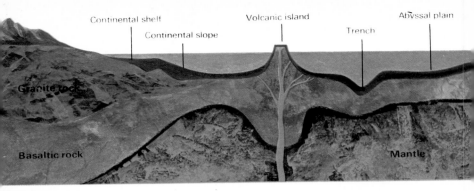

Continental shelf
Continental slope
Volcanic island
Trench
Abyssal plain
Granite rock
Basaltic rock
Mantle

Cross section of the ocean floor showing some of its variations.

lems, but now there are many scientific instruments which can be used for obtaining information. For example, the relief of the sea-bed can be determined by sonar equipment which sends out sound waves to hit the sea-bed and bounce back again to special recording equipment.

One of the many mysteries of the sea concerns canyons which occur off many river mouths such as the Hudson and Zaire. These were thought to be old river valleys which had been flooded because of rising sea level or sinking of land, but as they are sometimes as much as 400 or 500 metres deep, another explanation seems necessary. The most likely involves *turbidity currents*. These are movements of very muddy water which slide over the sea-bed like an avalanche and rush down continental slopes with great erosive power. You can see the way

these currents operate by doing a simple experiment. Pour some coloured liquid into a bath containing water and watch the way it flows beneath the surface in a distinctive movement before it begins to merge with the other water.

Below are diagrams to show Mount Everest in relation to the depth dived by the bathysphere *Trieste* (*right*) into the Marianas Trench in 1953. The Trieste was designed by Auguste Piccard.

8708 m

10692 m

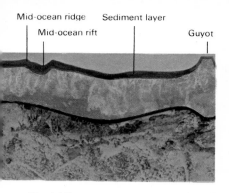

Mid-ocean ridge   Sediment layer

Mid-ocean rift   Guyot

Turbidity currents are associated with a large amount of muddy sediment, but elsewhere in the ocean material is being deposited. All over the oceans, sediment is accumulating on the ocean floor. This sediment may have come from the land (*terrigenous*) as broken up fragments of rock, or from the sea (*pelagic*) as remains of dead sea creatures. Near the land the sediment consists mostly of sands and clays of terrigenous origin, but away from the coastlines it is mainly pelagic.

These deep water sediments are called *oozes*. They consist of millions of tiny dead creatures, broken down fragments of shells and skeletons of larger animals. The remains may be *calcareous* or *siliceous* in character. Calcareous oozes are called *globigerina* or *pteropod*, and siliceous oozes are *diatom* and *radiolarian*. These occur over vast expanses of the ocean, as shown in the illustration.

Red clay deposits, predominate in

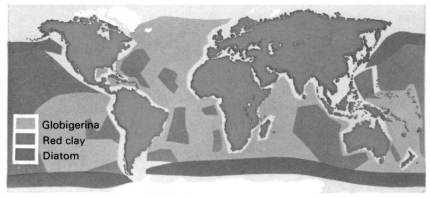

Globigerina
Red clay
Diatom

Map to show distribution of common deposits on the ocean floor.

the ocean deeps because the calcareous and siliceous remains are dissolved and hence do not fall to the sea bed. This clay is thought to be the accumulation of dust particles which have circled the earth after volcanic eruptions. This dust would have fallen on the land masses and in shallow sea areas as well, but in these areas the clay has been lost in the midst of other thicker deposits. It is only in the deepest parts of the ocean, where there are no other deposits, that the red clay can be seen.

The water in the oceans contains dissolved salts as well as the sediment. The degree of saltiness is called the *salinity* of the water and this varies from place to place. The average salinity of the oceans is 35 parts per 1000, or 35‰. This figure is based on the fact that 1000 lb (453 kg) of water contains 35 lb (15 kg) of salts. At the equator the salinity is only 34‰ because the heavy rainfall adds to the amount of water, thereby reducing the proportion of salt. Near the tropics where the temperatures are high but the rainfall is low, the figure is 36‰. The Mediterranean Sea is in a warm area and so evaporation is high; rainfall is low and there are few large rivers to bring in fresh water. So, the average salinity there is up to 40‰. The Baltic Sea on the other hand is in a cool area with little evaporation, and many large rivers bring supplies of fresh water. Thus the salinity is less than 20‰ and as low as 2‰ in the northern parts of the Gulf of Bothnia.

Just as salinity varies from one place to another, so too do the temperatures. The sun is the major source of heat, and in the tropical latitude, where it is always vertical, it gives much more heat than anywhere else. Accordingly, the oceanic temperatures decrease steadily from

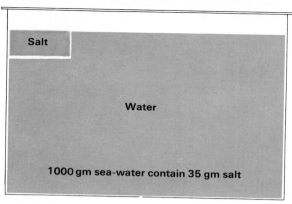

The proportion of salts in the oceanic water.

the equator to the poles. Average temperatures near the equator are about 25°C and slightly higher in certain areas such as the Gulf of Mexico. In temperate latitudes – for example, near Britain – temperatures range from 17°C or 18°C in

summer to as low as 10°C off southern England in winter, or only 6°C off north-east Scotland.

The steady decrease in temperature from the equator to the poles is upset by ocean currents which transfer vast quantities of water from one latitude to another. For example, the Gulf Stream carries warm water into the North Atlantic from the Gulf of Mexico. It comes to Europe as the North Atlantic Drift, and makes the Atlantic off Europe

Average distribution of temperatures throughout the world.

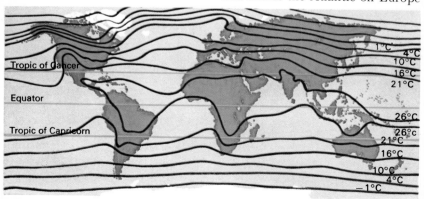

The main ocean currents of the North Atlantic. There is a clockwise circulation north of the equator.

much warmer than it should be for its latitude. The western Atlantic off the coast of Canada is much cooler than one would expect for its latitude because of the influence of the Labrador Current. This is a flow of cold water coming from the ice-bound seas off western Greenland.

Ocean currents are caused by winds, the rotation of the earth and the shape of the land. In the Atlantic, the equatorial currents flow from east to west because they are blown by the trade winds. The North Equatorial current then turns to its right because of the effect of the rotation of the earth, whereas the South Equatorial current turns to its left. In the South Atlantic, the effect of the earth's rotation gives an anti-clockwise flow of currents, but in the North Atlantic there is a clockwise circulation. Currents such as the Canary and Benguela are both cold, because they are flowing towards the equator. As they are flowing from cooler into warmer latitudes, they are colder than the surrounding water. They are also cooled by water which upwells from beneath the surface of the ocean in order to replace the top layer of water blown westwards by the trade winds.

In addition to ocean currents there are movements associated with tides. It is the gravitational attraction of the sun and the moon which causes the tides. The pull of the moon is stronger than that of the sun, because it is so much nearer. If the sun and the moon are acting together, very high tides, called *spring tides*, result. If the sun and the moon are neutralising each other, tides are much lower, and are called *neap tides*.

There are some peculiarities of tides which cannot be explained, however. Most of Britain has two high tides and two low tides every 24 hours, or 24 hours 50 minutes, to be precise. Each tide is about 25 minutes later than the previous one because the moon has moved its position and influence. Southampton and the surrounding area has an extended high tide for reasons not yet fully understood, and the Mediterranean has virtually no tides. Tahiti experiences high tides at midday and midnight, which suggests that they are controlled more by the sun than the moon.

Moon and sun working together cause spring tides (*left*) and neutralising each other cause neap tides (*right*).

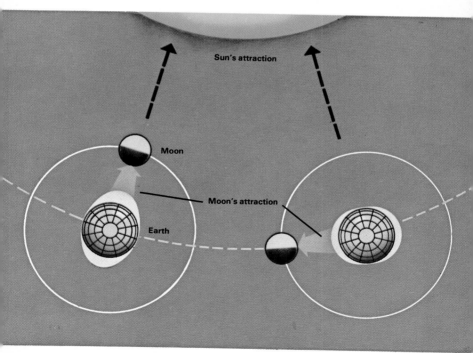

25

The Land Masses

The word *geomorphology* means the study of the surface features of the earth. It is that branch of geography which studies the landscape. It attempts to explain why in some places hills occur, but in others plateaux and plains are found and why some hills are much steeper than others.

As a result of earth movements, new mountains are being formed all the time, although the process is too slow to be seen during the life span of a human being. As the mountains are being uplifted, erosion by rivers, ice, snow and other agents begins to wear them away. Eventually, if the upward movement ceases for a long period of millions of years, the mountains will be worn down to sea level. The eroded material is washed into rivers and then carried to the sea, where it accumulates as sediment on the sea floor. These sediments, after a considerable period of time, are compressed into rocks and will be uplifted to form new mountains, which will be attacked by the agents of erosion. This slow, continuous process whereby rocks are uplifted, worn away, deposited in the sea and then uplifted again, is called the *cycle of erosion*. It has been carrying on in this way for millions of years.

Rock cycle shows rocks being eroded, transported, deposited and then uplifted.

Rocks

One very important aspect of geomorphology is the rock type. There are three groups of rocks – *igneous, sedimentary*, and *metamorphic* – and all rocks belong to one or other of these groups. A rock is simply defined as a collection of minerals.

The word igneous, comes from the Latin word *ignis* for fire; igneous rocks originate from volcanic activity. When formed, these rocks are very hot and liquid, but as they cool the minerals begin to solidify, though not all at the same time. If the molten rock, or *magma*, reaches the surface of the earth, it will cool quite quickly and the chemicals will solidify or crystallize into small minerals. If the magma stays below the surface it will cool rather more slowly and small minerals of one type will have time to merge with other minerals of the same type; larger crystals will result in this case. Examining crystals, then, is the best method for distinguishing between igneous rocks which formed on the surface and those which formed underground.

The second important method of identifying igneous rocks is based on mineral content. Some rocks contain a high proportion of silica and feldspar – these are called *acidic rocks*. Others containing little silica but many ferro-magnesian minerals are called *basic rocks*. Half-way between acidic and basic rocks is another category – the *intermediate rocks*. Acidic rocks tend to be light in

Sedimentary rocks on the coast of southern England.

colour, whereas basic rocks are much darker. Igneous rocks can be identified by their crystal size and colour. For example, a large-grained light-coloured rock is granite, while a small-grained dark green or black rock is basalt.

The sedimentary rocks are derived from eroded fragments of existing rocks. The particles are carried to the sea by rivers and there they mix with particles of dead sea creatures. When rivers reach the sea their speed of flow is reduced, and they then lose their carrying power and deposit sediment. They drop the large particles first and the smallest last. In the shallowest water, mainly coarse gravel and sand are found. Further out clays occur and gradually, as land-derived sediment diminishes, cal-

27

careous remnants of animals become dominant. In the deeper water limestones form, in the muddy areas clays, and in the shallower water sandstones. If the limestones contain little land sediment, and are therefore pure calcium carbonate, they will be called *chalk*.

The third group of rocks are those which have been changed or have undergone metamorphism. Once either igneous or sedimentary rocks, they have been changed by heat or pressure. The heat comes from volcanic activity and the pressure from the folding of rocks. The most effective metamorphism occurs when folding and volcanic activity coincide. Crystals may be changed, frequently being stretched out or elongated by the effects of heat or pressure. This gives rise to layered or banded rocks. *Schist* and *gneiss* are two examples of rocks which were once igneous and were then changed. Slate is clay which has been metamorphosed, and marble is metamorphosed limestone. Metamorphic rocks are often hard, and are generally associated with high and rugged scenery. They are often quarried for building stone or broken into gravel-sized pieces to make foundations for roads (road metal).

Metamorphic rocks occur near igneous intrusions and in the midst of folded strata where the pressure is great.

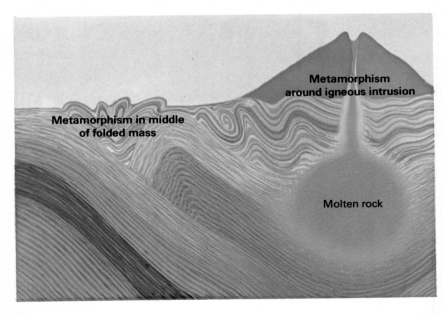

Metamorphism around igneous intrusion

Metamorphism in middle of folded mass

Molten rock

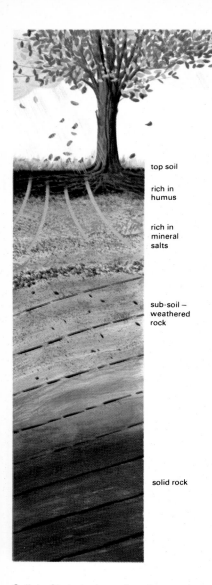

top soil

rich in humus

rich in mineral salts

sub-soil – weathered rock

solid rock

Soil profile in moist region. Arrows show the direction of water movement.

Soils

Rocks are gradually broken down into smaller fragments by weathering. A layer of rock fragments is called *regolith* and supports a few primitive plants such as moss and lichens which provide humus. The regolith particles combine with humus to form soil in which a variety of plants will grow. These plants will help to develop the soils, and layers or *horizons* will be created, as shown in the illustration. 'A' is the top soil and 'D' is the bedrock.

The character of the soil will be determined by the rock type, and also by climate which controls the type of weathering.

On limestone rocks the soil will be very alkaline, while on granite the soil will be coarse and acidic. Clay soils are obviously very different from sandy soils. In areas of heavy rainfall, chemicals may be washed away and soils are deprived of useful constituents; soils in humid areas are therefore quite different from desert soils.

Where coniferous trees grow, the needles fall to the ground and create an acidic, greyish soil known by the Russian name of *podzol*.

The world's grasslands, such as the Prairies, contain soils which are blackened by the mass of grass roots. The soils are called *blackearths* or *chernozems*. In areas of extensive deciduous forest such as Britain used to be, grey-brown forest soils have been created by rotting humus and leaves.

Structures

Rocks which make up the surface of the earth are continuously subjected to erosion as well as uplift and movement. The earth movements which cause uplift of mountain ranges and plateaux are called *tectonic movements*. A layer of rock is named a *stratum*, and as these strata are uplifted by tectonic movements they may be bent or broken. Bending is termed *folding* and breaking is called *faulting*. Folding may be simple and symmetrical, although it is more frequently lopsided or asymmetrical. The folds may be pushed right over, in which case they are called *recumbent folds*. The upfold is called an *anticline* and the downfold a *syncline*.

Highest and lowest places.

The rocks subjected to earth movements may suffer from faulting in which the strata break, and may move up or down in relation to adjacent rocks. The faults may be normal or reverse, but if several occur in close proximity they may create elevated or downthrown land. Land which has risen between two or more faults is called a *horst* or block mountain of which the Grampians, Massif Central, Meseta and Vosges are examples. Land which has subsided between faults is called a *graben* or rift valley, such as Central Valley of Scotland, the Great Glen including Loch Ness, the Rhine Valley between the Vosges and Black Mountains, and the Great Rift Valley of East Africa.

Mountain building and earth movements are associated with the

Highest Mountains – Asia

	Metres
Everest	8853
K 2 (Godwin Austen)	8616
Kangchenjunga	8591
Makalu	8480
Dhaulagiri	8177
Nanga Parbat	8131
Annapurna	8083

plus 17 more before Aconcagua, the highest in the world outside Asia.

Highest Mountains – Other

Country/Continent	Mountain	Metres
S. America	Aconcagua	6964
	Llullaillaco	6925
	Illimani	6886
Africa	Kilimanjaro	5898
Antarctica	Vinson Massif	5143
Australia	Mt Kosciusko	2231
New Zealand	Mt Cook	3766

Country/Continent	Mountain	Metres
Europe	Mt Elbrus	5637
Europe (excl. Caucasus)	Mt Blanc	4813
N. America	Mt McKinley	6197
Mainland U.S.A.	Mt Whitney	4420
Britain	Ben Nevis	1343
Wales	Snowdon	1085
England	Scafell	979
Ireland	Macgillicuddy	1041

Greatest Mountain

Mauna Kea	10210
(above sea level)	4207

Lowest Places on Land

Dead Sea		−396
Africa	L. Assal	−150
N. America	Death Valley	−86
S. America	Salinas Grandes	−39·9
Australia	L. Eyre	−15

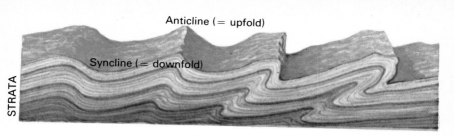

Anticline (= upfold)

Syncline (= downfold)

STRATA

Symmetric folding on the left and asymmetric folding on the right.

earth's plates, convection currents and continental drift. Mountains which were formed quite recently, that is within the Tertiary era during the last 40 million years, tend to be high and rugged, and include the Alps, Himalayas, Rockies and Andes. These are called *young fold*

Faulted structures. Faulting scrapes the rocks to form slickensides.

mountains and the period of formation is called the Alpine. Older mountains which were uplifted at any time during the Mesozoic, Palaeozoic or Pre-Cambrian geological eras are all gathered together under the name of *old fold mountains*.

The main periods of formation are called Hercynian (about 300 million years ago) and Caledonian (about 400 million years ago). These mountains have been worn down by erosion for so long that they are normally lower and

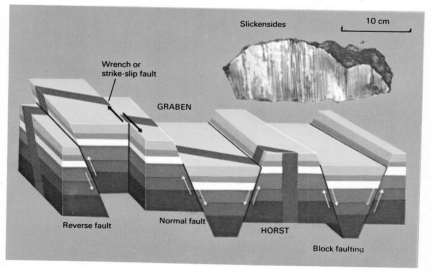

Slickensides

10 cm

Wrench or strike-slip fault

GRABEN

Reverse fault

Normal fault

HORST

Block faulting

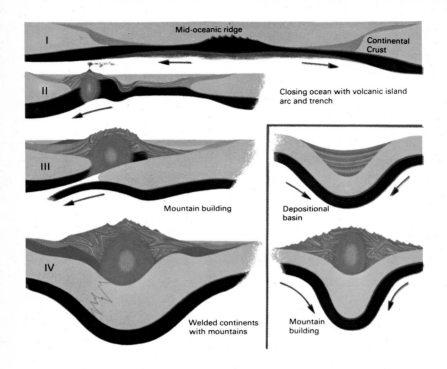

I

Mid-oceanic ridge

Continental Crust

II

Closing ocean with volcanic island arc and trench

III

Mountain building

Depositional basin

IV

Welded continents with mountains

Mountain building

I–IV show mountain building by plate tectonics, the modern explanation. The old explanation is shown in the inset. Here the crust subsides and sediments are compressed and folded.

smoother than young fold mountains. Examples include the Scottish and Welsh Highlands, the mountains of Norway, the Appalachians and the Great Dividing Ranges of Australia.

All highland areas are not fold mountains, however. Some may be horsts or other plateaux. Bolivia and Tibet are both situated on plateaux though surrounded by much higher mountains, and these are called *inter-montane* plateaux. The Deccan in India and much of Washington and Oregon in northwest U.S.A. have been built up by numerous fissure eruptions. A fissure is merely a crack in the surface rocks through which very fluid, basic lava flows and spreads out over the surrounding landscape. Both in the Deccan and north-west U.S.A., the lavas cover an area of 500 000 square kilometres and attain thicknesses of 2000 metres.

Denudation

Denudation will involve erosion, weathering and transportation. Without the effects of transportation all the broken down fragments of rock would stay in their areas of origin and protect those areas from subsequent erosion. Transport of eroded or weathered material may be caused by several things: gradient, whereby rocks may slide or slip down hill, river action, ice action or even wind action.

Weathering is the break-up or disintegration of rock on the spot by weather, without any outside influences from movements of water and so on. Weathering may be mechanical, chemical or biological. Mechanical or physical weathering is mainly caused by freeze and thaw action; chemical weathering is caused by dilute acids and water making the rocks decay; and biological weathering is the result of plants or animals breaking open the rocks.

Erosion is the break-up of rocks by moving agents such as running water, ice, wind or waves. It may be physical or chemical. Physical erosion is also known as *corrosion*, and chemical erosion includes both solution and carbonation. Rates of erosion depend on rock type and the chemicals within the rock. Lines of weakness, such as joints, will enable weathering to attack rocks which are hard, such as granite. Poorly cemented rocks will also decay quickly, even though the mineral particles themselves are hard. Rates of erosion also depend on climate. Hot and wet tropical climates cause rapid chemical disintegration of rocks, whereas in high mountain areas the mechanical action of freezing and thawing is most effective. In mild, humid Britain rivers are most active at present, though freeze and thaw continue to weather the highlands. During the last 2 million years, glaciers have also been active in the British Isles.

A family tree to show the different agents of denudation.

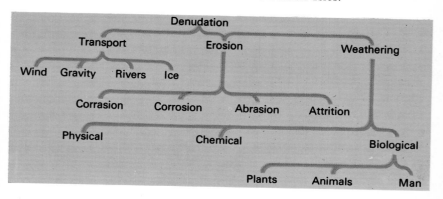

33

Earthquakes

Earthquakes are caused by underground movements associated with activity along plate boundaries. These movements create shaking or trembling which transmits shock waves through the rocks. They may originate several kilometres below the surface at a point known as the focus. The location on the earth's surface directly above the focus is called the *epicentre*.

The amount of damage caused by an earthquake may be plotted on a map, and lines can be drawn through places where shaking and damage are approximately equal. These are known as *isoseismal lines*. A seismograph is the instrument which records the amount of shaking, and there are now international scales to show the intensity of the earthquake. One scale is called the Rossi-Forel and, whereas point 1 on the scale would pass almost unnoticed, point 5 would see furniture disturbed, point 7 leads to panic as walls begin to crack, and point 10 equals widespread destruction. Another commonly used scale is the Richter, in which a magnitude of $7 \cdot 0$ is a major earthquake and $8 \cdot 6$ is the greatest ever recorded.

Most of the world's earthquakes occur in three main areas: in a line extending through Eurasia from the Mediterranean Sea to China; on mid-oceanic ridges; and around the edge of the Pacific Ocean. This last area, the circum-Pacific belt, is the most active part of the world, both for volcanoes and earthquakes.

When the stresses and strains within the crust eventually cause the earthquake, waves travel through the rocks from the focus. These shock waves are initially of two types: 1. primary (P) or longitudinal waves, sometimes known as *push waves*. These travel straight through the rocks in a similar fash-

Principal earthquake and volcanic zones throughout the world.

Earthquakes
Volcanoes

Four storey brick building in Gediz (Turkey), destroyed by aftershocks of an earthquake in March, 1970.

ion to sound waves travelling through air, and they can pass through liquids and solids. 2. secondary (S) or transverse waves, sometimes known as *shove waves*. These travel like light waves, somewhat similar to the snake-like action created by holding one end of a piece of rope and shaking it.

S waves only pass through solids, and it was information from P and S waves which revealed that the centre of the earth was liquid. When P and S waves reach the surface they create longitudinal (L) waves. These are the slowest but the most destructive as they pass through the surface rocks of the earth, with decreasing power away from the epicentre. Earthquakes can cause terrible devastation and may even destroy complete towns. For instance, the San Francisco earthquake of 1906 demolished many of the buildings. Agadir in Morocco was flattened in 1960, and a 1976 earthquake near Tangshan in northern China may have killed nearly 1 million people. Scientists are trying to predict earthquakes so that people will be able to escape before the shock waves strike.

Volcanoes

Volcanic activity is caused by underground movements similar to those which create earthquakes. This is why volcanoes and earthquakes often occur in the same places. Volcanoes may result from two plates moving away from each other, which will allow lavas to flow out on to the earth's surface, or they may result from two plates colliding and one sinking beneath the other. The collision of plates causes more vibrant eruptive activity and deep-focused earthquakes.

There are approximately 700 active volcanoes at present. The exact number is not known because it is not always clear if a volcano is merely dormant or whether it has become extinct. Also, a volcano may be so large that it has several craters. In this case, does it count as only one volcano?

Most of the world's volcanoes are located in the circum-Pacific belt and the mid-world belt, extending through the Middle East from the Alps to China. There are a few active volcanoes along the mid-Atlantic ridge, in the West Indies,

Types of lava and fumaroles (steam volcanoes).

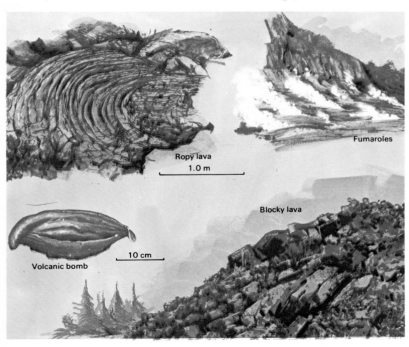

Fumaroles

Ropy lava
1.0 m

Blocky lava

Volcanic bomb
10 cm

An erupting volcano with a main crater and two subsidiary vents.

and near the Great African Rift Valley.

When volcanic activity begins there may be violent explosions blowing out gases, dust and rocks: or there may be quieter outpourings of lava. The molten rock is known as *magma*. Sometimes it does not reach the surface, and in this case it would be known as an *intrusive rock* when it cooled and solidified. Intrusions may cover many kilometres and are known as *batholiths*. Although formed beneath the surface, they may be exposed by erosion of the overlying rock. If the area of intrusive rock is more than 100 km² it is known as a batholith, but, if smaller, it is known as a *stock* or a *boss*.

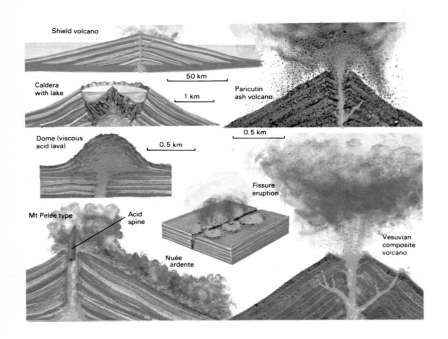

Labels on figure:
Shield volcano
Caldera with lake
Dome (viscous acid lava)
Mt Pelée type
Acid spine
Nuée ardente
Paricutin ash volcano
Fissure eruption
Vesuvian composite volcano
50 km
1 km
0.5 km
0.5 km
0.5 km

The most common shapes and types of volcanoes.

Dartmoor is an example of a boss. Laccoliths, lopoliths, phacoliths, sills and dykes are other examples of intrusive rocks. If lava reaches the surface in molten form it solidifies as an *extrusive rock*. The lavas may be acidic, basic or intermediate. If they are basic, the lava is free-flowing and may travel at 4–6 km/h; but if acidic, the movement is slow, as the lava is very thick and viscous. Acidic volcanoes are steep-sided, whereas basic lavas give more gentle slopes.

After an outpouring of lava has ceased, the volcano may have to explode to create another opening for the next flow of lava. This explosion blows out dust and fragments of rock into the air, and they fall back to land and help to build up a mountain. This is why volcanoes are often layered with lava followed by explosive material. The explosion blows out material known collectively as *pyroclasts* or *tephra*. They include breccia, pumice and scoriae which are lumps of rock, volcanic bombs which are lumps of lava, and tuff which is ash and dust. There are also gases and water associated with the explosion. The water will often contribute to the heavy rainfall associated with eruptions. This rain may mix with volcanic dust to form a mud river such as that which covered Herculaneum after the Vesuvius eruption of A.D. 79. Pompeii was buried in the same eruption, by ash instead of mud. Gases may also be devastating, as poisonous, hot clouds may roll down volcanoes after eruption. They are called *nuées ardentes*, and one such cloud killed nearly everyone in the town of St Pierre on the island of Martinique after Mont Pelée erupted in 1902. The only survivor in the town was a man in prison awaiting execution.

Another famous and devastating volcanic eruption was that of Krakatoa which, like Mont Pelée, killed over 30 000 people. It exploded in 1883 with one of the loudest noises ever heard on earth, and although the eruption contributed to the deaths, it was the effect of the tidal waves which was most disastrous. Submarine earthquakes and volcanoes send out ripples across the sea similar to the ripples created by throwing a stone into a pond. These ripples travel fairly harmlessly across oceans at more than 600 km/h, but on entering shallow water and approaching coastlines they pile up and create large waves 10 metres in height, which crash on to the shore, causing total destruction. These tidal waves are not connected with tides and are now

Hot-springs in Turkey with people bathing on the top terrace. Chemicals in the water solidify to form the platforms.

generally known by the Japanese name *tsunamis*. The tsunamis caused after Krakatoa drowned over 30 000 people and threw ocean-going vessels up on to the land.

After an eruption, geysers or mud springs may be left behind as signs of dying volcanic activity. Other evidence is also left behind in the shape of volcanic mountains and the volcanic necks or remaining stumps of very ancient volcanoes, as at Le Puy in France or Edinburgh Castle rock in Scotland.

Rivers

It is difficult measuring the lengths of rivers because it is impossible to determine exactly where they end. Also, they change. For example, the Nile became shorter when Lake Nasser extended across many old meanders and straightened the course of the river.

Rivers are very important, not only as movers of water from land to sea, but also as sculptors of the landscape. Many features of the countryside have been shaped by rivers. All rivers erode and deposit, with erosion occurring more in mountainous areas and deposition near the coast. Rivers are also great transporters of material – the Mississippi, for example, has been estimated to carry over 500 million tonnes of sediment to the sea annually.

Longest rivers, biggest river basins and largest delta.

In hilly regions, rivers tend to be fairly straight and have pebbly beds. The water is clear because of the absence of fine mud particles. Pot holes are eroded on the bed of the river, and these contribute to the vertical or downward erosion which is typical. This is why the valley in cross-section will be steep and roughly V-shaped. As the river reaches lower ground, although its speed of flow remains the same, it begins to meander. The meanders wander around *spurs*, which are higher areas protruding into the valley. The outside bend of the river erodes the valley wall, thereby widening the valley into a more flattened U shape. This lateral erosion by the meanders erodes the valley sides into steep walls which are called *bluffs* or *meander scars*. While erosion occurs on the outside of the bends, on the insides where the current is weaker there is deposition

Longest Rivers in the World

	Km
Nile	6673
Amazon	6520
Mississippi Missouri	6053
Irtysh	5152
Yangtze	4991
Amur	4669
Zaire	4347
Hwang	4347
Lena	4258
Mackenzie	4242
Mekong	4186
Niger	4186
Yenisey	3799
Murray Darling	3719

Longest River in Europe

Danube	2849

Longest River in Britain

Shannon	386

Longest River in U.K.

Severn	354

Longest River in England

Thames	346

River with the Greatest Flow

Amazon	average	4 200 000 cu secs
Amazon	in flood	7 000 000 cu secs

Biggest River Basins

Amazon Basin	covers	7 044 000 sq km
Shannon Basin		15 695 sq km
Severn Basin		11 419 sq km

Largest Delta

Ganges-Brahmaputra	77 700 sq km

Grand Falls, Arizona. Horizontal rock strata form the largest waterfalls.

which helps to build up a flood plain. Moving on down the river, the meanders become larger, the valley much wider and the valley walls gentle, or almost non-existent. A flattened U-shaped cross-section results.

As the meanders wander aimlessly across the flood plain, they often become so twisted that they cut themselves off to form *oxbow lakes*, which are fragments of old meanders. These will eventually dry up, but may remain as marshy

Narrow V shaped and a wider U shaped valley.

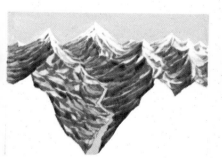

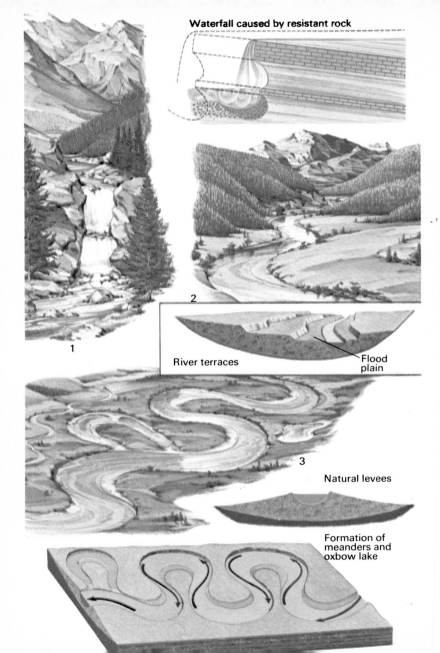

Waterfall caused by resistant rock

River terraces

Flood plain

Natural levees

Formation of meanders and oxbow lake

1

2

3

patches for many years. River floods spreading out across the plain fill up these hollows with sediment. The sediment accumulates most rapidly near the river, and thus enlarged banks are built up. These are called *levees*, and alongside the Mississippi there are some which reach 15 metres in height. Deposits are also laid down on the bed of the river and so it is possible for the river to become higher than the surrounding flood plain, from which it is separated only by levees. If the river then floods the effect is disastrous. The Hwang and the Po are two rivers which have broken through levees and flooded thousands of hectares of land. In 1852 the Hwang drowned 1 million people and changed its course by 480 kilometres as a result of one flood.

If the rock over which a river is flowing is of uniform type, the river's course is quite smooth, but irregularities occur with variations of rock type. Harder rocks are eroded more slowly than soft rocks and this creates rapids and waterfalls. If the stratum of hard rock is vertical, only a small fall will result, but if there is a horizontal layer then a large fall may form. If this happens, the fall will be undercut, will then collapse and gradually retreat upstream, leaving a gorge behind.

The development of river scenery: 1. youthful river with steep valleys and waterfalls. 2. mature river cuts successive terraces. 3. senile river forms meanders and oxbow lakes.

This has happened at the famous Niagara Falls, Victoria Falls, and many other places.

At the source of a stream the rock is rotted away and transported downstream, and gradually the river works its way uphill. This is known as *headward erosion*. It sometimes happens that a river working back upstream may intercept, or capture, the water of a stream flowing in another direction. This is called *river capture* or river piracy, and gives one river extra water and extra powers of erosion. Uplift of land near the source, or lowering of sea level, may also give a river increased powers of erosion. This increased power is called *rejuvenation* and may cause meanders to be cut much deeper. These are called *incised meanders*, and can be seen on many rivers, such as the Dee in Wales or the Wear at Durham. The old flood plain may be abandoned and a new plain created at a lower level, as a result of renewed erosion. The old flood plain would become a river terrace.

When the river reaches the sea it may flow into an estuary or it may build a delta. The Amazon has both, with an estuary of over 100 metres deep and large deltaic islands. Large deltas are found at the mouths of the Ganges, Niger, Nile and Mississippi. The Nile delta is almost triangular in shape. This is the shape of a Greek capital D which is called 'delta' and has given its name to all river deltas.

Glaciation

Snow is formed by tiny ice crystals joining together to make a flake, and if the snow falls in an area with sub-zero temperatures, it will steadily accumulate. Snowflakes contain air but, as more pile up, the weight compresses the snow beneath and squeezes out the air. This compressed snow is called *névé* or *firn*. Increasing pressure on the névé will remove all air and will produce ice, which is bluish in colour. If enough ice is formed, then an ice sheet or ice cap will result.

An ice sheet is a vast expanse of ice covering hills and valleys, as in Antarctica or Greenland at the present time, or in Britain 1 million years ago. An ice cap is a small ice sheet such as may be found in Iceland, Norway or the Alps. During the Ice Age, which lasted from 2 million years ago until about 10 000 B.C., ice sheets covered lowlands in Europe and North America. We are now living in a warmer phase, and snow and ice are restricted to the highlands.

Surplus ice from the ice caps still moves towards the lowlands, but only as tongues or rivers of ice, and not as ice sheets. These ribbons of surplus ice slide down existing river valleys and are called *glaciers*. Glaciers are caused by pressure

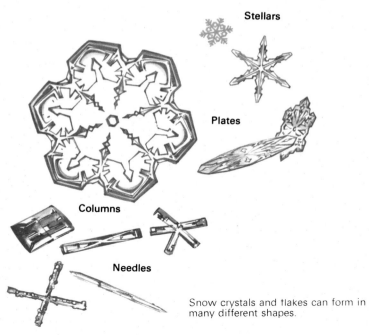

Stellars

Plates

Columns

Needles

Snow crystals and flakes can form in many different shapes.

Polar bears on pack ice between Alaska and Siberia.

squeezing surplus ice downhill. They extend beyond the snow line, which is the limit of land covered by permanent snow and ice. At the downstream end of a glacier the ice is melting, which is why glaciers always have rivers flowing from them. The loss of ice at the end of the glacier is replaced by more ice pushing down the valley. If the replacement rate is less than the melt rate, the glacier will shrink and appear to retreat uphill. This is what happens in summer. In winter the replacement rate is greater than the melt rate and the ice will advance.

The speed of movement in most glaciers is only a few centimetres a day, but in Greenland some glaciers advance by as much as 30 metres a day. As they move they crack and open up to form *crevasses* which are very dangerous. Mountaineers would never walk near crevasses unless they were roped together.

Glaciers advance and retreat with seasonal changes of temperature,

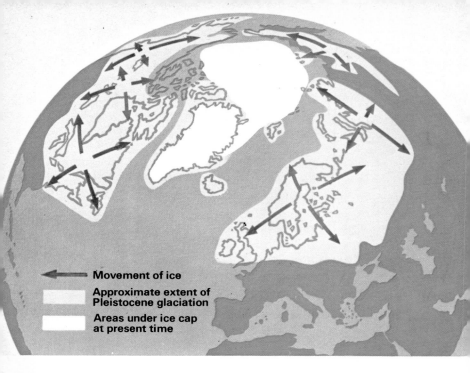

Movement of ice

**Approximate extent of
Pleistocene glaciation**

**Areas under ice cap
at present time**

Map to show present ice cover and the
maximum extent of the ice cover during
the Pleistocene Ice Age.

just as the ice sheets of the Pleistocene Ice Age moved. The ice advances were called *glacials* and the periods of retreat *interglacials*. There were several glacial and interglacial periods during the Pleistocene, which started 2 million years ago, and we may now be living in an interglacial period. It is not fully understood why the Ice Age started, or how many glacial advances there were – which is why many scientists are studying the period. Expedi-

tions frequently go to Greenland and Antarctica to do research in those areas.

The major ice accumulations are in mountainous areas, as shown by present day conditions in the Alps, the South Island of New Zealand, Alaska and elsewhere. The ice cap provides the snow and the ice which forms the glaciers. Above the snow there are isolated mountain peaks which suffer from freezing and thawing activity. The rocks freeze at night and thaw during the day. When they freeze, the water within them expands by 9% of its volume, and then contracts again during the day. The expansion and contraction breaks the rock into fragments which then fall down the hillside onto the glaciers. Millions of these fragments turn the ice into a very coarse form of sandpaper, which can scrape away at the rocks. As the ice moves it widens, deepens, and straightens valleys and converts old V-shaped river valleys into U-shaped glacial valleys. In glacial areas the ice in the valleys has eroded the spurs and created truncated spurs which have steep slopes

A mountainous area which has been affected by glaciation.

looking over the valley. These are often used by rock climbers.

Old tributary valleys may be left at a higher level, as a result of the deepening of the main valley. These become *hanging valleys*, and often have large waterfalls dropping down to the main valley, as in Lauterbrunnen in Switzerland or Yosemite in California. In Britain, most of the hanging valleys merely contain fast-flowing, tumbling streams. At the head of the glacial valley there is a large armchair hollow called a *corrie* (Scotland) *cwm* (Wales) or *cirque* (France), which was once the source of the glacier. A

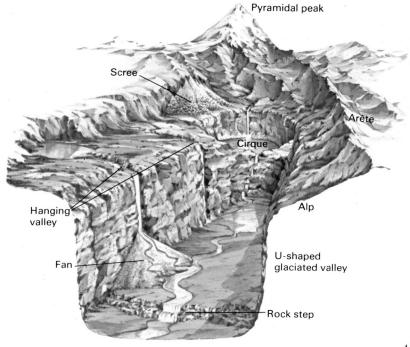

Pyramidal peak

Scree

Arête

Cirque

Hanging valley

Alp

Fan

U-shaped glaciated valley

Rock step

47

narrow knife-edged ridge separating two corries is called an *arête*, and if a complete mountain side has been eroded by several corries, a pyramidal peak or horn will result.

As glaciers travel, they erode and also transport large quantities of rock. Some particles may be large boulders, but much is fine dust, rock flour or clay. This material will gradually fall through the ice to reach the valley floor, and will all be deposited on the floor when the ice finally melts. Deposition of material tends to take place in the lower areas, whereas erosion is more active in the highlands.

Large fragments of rock deposited by ice are called *moraine*. Morainic material may be pushed to the side of the valley by the movements of the ice (lateral moraine), pushed down the valley to the end of the ice (terminal moraine), left on the valley floor (ground moraine), or may be located in the middle of the ice if two glaciers have merged (medial moraine). Fine particles of rock deposited by ice are called *till* or *boulder clay*, and consist of clay, some sands and some larger rocks. Till is found in most glacial valleys, but also over large expanses of country as a result of ice sheets. Such areas can be seen in East Yorkshire, north Germany and central U.S.A. Mounds of till may form hillocks up to 15 metres in height, and these are

A collection of features of glacial deposition.

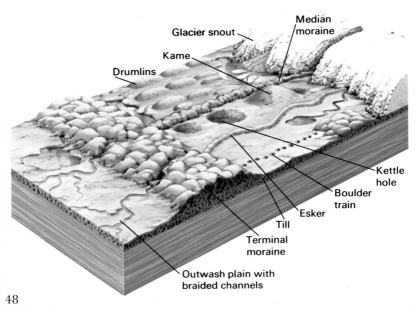

Median moraine

Glacier snout

Kame

Drumlins

Kettle hole

Boulder train

Esker

Till

Terminal moraine

Outwash plain with braided channels

A Norwegian fjord showing the steep walls of an ice cut valley.

called *drumlins*.

Other small mounds and ridges are formed underneath the ice by the action of running water. All glaciers have water flowing on and underneath them, as the speed of movement prevents freezing. These streams deposit sands and gravels which become exposed when the ice melts. Elongated ridges are called *eskers*, and patches or mounds of sand and gravel are called *kames*. Blocks of ice may be left behind in the kames or in till deposits, and when they finally melt they leave hollows which are called *kettle holes*. Beyond the terminal moraine there may also be other deposits of sand and gravel, washed away by melt water streams. These deposits are called *outwash sands*. The southern part of Long Island, New York, is an outwash plain.

Coastlines

All coastlines are different because no two stretches of coast have exactly the same rock type, climatic and weather conditions or position. Many coastlines do show some similarities, however. Coastlines may be highland or lowland, erosional or depositional, submerging or emerging, or a combination of these. Coastlines of submergence will normally be indented and irregular with rias (flooded river valleys) and wide estuaries. Offshore islands will be quite common as they will be the remnants of old hill summits. Where mountain ranges which run parallel to the coast have been submerged, as in Yugoslavia, British Columbia or Southern Chile, the resultant coastline will be very different from coastlines in areas where the mountain ranges are at right angles to the coast, as in south-west Ireland. Coastlines of emergence will generally contain a wide coastal plain, as in eastern U.S.A., with raised beaches and caves occurring inland. Coastlines are normally irregular if erosion is taking place, though they may be straight in areas of deposition.

If coastlines contain different rock types, there will be different rates of erosion and the softer rocks will be worn back more quickly than hard rocks. Whether a rock is soft or hard may depend on the rocks which surround it. For example, limestone situated between outcrops of clay or soft sandstone would be regarded as hard and would form a peninsula, whilst the clay or sandstone would be eroded more quickly to form inlets. If the same limestone was bordered by granite, or any very hard igneous rock, it would be regarded as soft. In this case, the limestone would be eroded more quickly than the granite, and would form an inlet.

No matter what rock type forms a peninsula or promontory, the waves can still attack the sides and open up joints to form caves. The lines of weakness will allow erosion of even the hardest rocks and so, eventually, all rocks will be worn away by the action of the sea. The sea can also erode by hydraulic action when air is trapped in hollows by the onrushing waves. The sand and shingle moved by the sea will help erosion too, as millions of particles are smashed into the rocks by the powerful effects of the waves. Sand particles have been hurled over 30 metres up cliffs on the coast of Scotland.

Headlands and promontories can be attacked by the sea from both sides, though one side will probably be subjected to a greater number of more powerful waves according to the prevailing wind direction. As the joints become caves and eventually tunnels, erosion may work upwards to the top of the peninsula to open up holes in the roofs of the caves. These holes may become blowholes with spray splashing up through them at high tide or when large waves are forced into the caves. Arches will form and eventually collapse, leaving an isolated pinnacle of rock. These island lumps, or small islands, are called *stacks* and are common on all rugged coastlines. Remnants of stacks may also occur on sandy beaches where they represent the last fragments and hardest parts of the former coastline.

Erosion of the coast will often

The Cornish coastline with sandy bays and rocky headlands.

Typical coastal features showing the results of erosion and deposition.

Labels on image: Bay with beach, Cave, Cliff, Arch, Stack, Wave-cut platform

form cliffs which may be several hundred metres in height. Cliffs in Chile and some in north-west Ireland exceed 600 metres. Large cliffs are generally formed of hard rocks though some, as in Yorkshire, consist of soft rocks such as clay. Since Roman times, the Yorkshire coast has retreated by 5 kilometres in places, whereas other cliffs have retreated by only a centimetre or two in the same 2000 years. Cliffs are not always vertical, especially in the case of softer rocks which will collapse more readily to give more gentle angles. Different angles occur on hard rock, too, depending on the

tilt of the strata. If the rocks are naturally dipping (or sloping) down to the sea they will give more gentle cliffs than those formed by rocks dipping inland, which may even give overhanging cliffs.

At the foot of cliffs the erosion will form a wave cut platform or *abrasion bench*, on which the eroded material will be deposited. Vast quantities of depositional rocks accumulate round coastlines, only to be broken up into smaller and smaller fragments by attrition. As the particles become smaller they can be carried along the shore by *longshore drift*. Longshore drift is a slow but continuous process. As a wave comes up the beach it will carry particles of sand along its line of travel, which is generally diagonal to the coastline. This movement of water up the beach is called *swash*, and when the water trickles back down the beach it is called backwash. The backwash is generally at right angles to the coastline so that the particles of sand swashed up the beach and backwashed down the beach will have travelled a short distance along the beach. This is longshore drift.

In order to reduce the movement of material along the coast, groynes are often constructed. These are generally wooden structures built out at right angles to the coast, and they trap much of the sand and shingle being carried along the shore. Material will pile up on one side of the groyne and eventually get washed over the top. Groynes will also take the main force of the waves, thereby protecting the coastline or sea wall from excessive damage. When longshore drift reaches inlets or estuaries, material is deposited in a line continuing the trend of the coastline. When this material builds up above sea level it is called a *spit*, examples of which can be seen on most coastlines. Behind the spit, marshes will occur and land reclamation may eventually take place.

If a spit extended right across an estuary, a delta would result.

Movements of grains of sand and pebbles along the shore and *below*, longshore drift builds spits across estuaries.

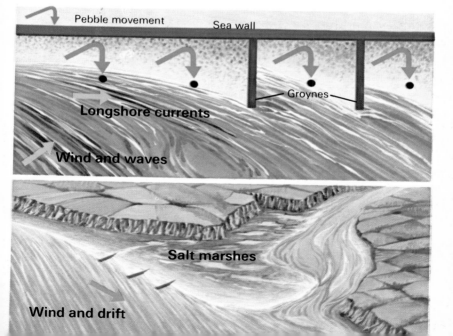

Arid Features

Arid areas, or deserts, are generally defined as those regions with less than 250 millimetres of rainfall in a year. The lack of rainfall means that there is little running water. Desert landscapes are often very steep and angular because there is no water to smooth the steep slopes by washing away sharp corners. Erosion in these areas is associated with changes of temperature. The land becomes very hot during the day – up to 60° or 70° centigrade. At this temperature the rocks may be too hot to touch, or even hot enough to fry an egg. During the night, temperatures often fall below freezing

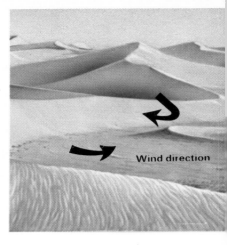

Wind direction

point. The expansion and contraction of rocks makes them split and large boulders break off. These boulders are then broken down into

Monument Valley in Arizona showing buttes (residual hills).

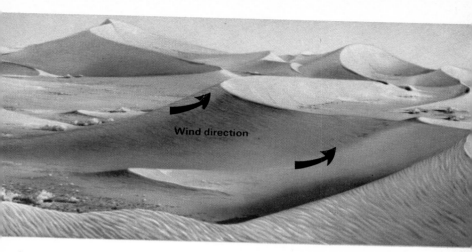

Sand dunes. The arrows show the wind direction.

smaller and smaller particles which eventually form sand.

As the landscape is weathered away, steep-sided, isolated hills remain. These are the relics of higher land, and are made of hard rocks which have been slowest to erode. These steep-sided rocks are like islands, and they are called *inselbergen*, from the German words for island and mountain. They are also called *residual hills*, as they are the residue or remnants of much bigger mountains.

The broken down fragments of rock eventually form the sand for which deserts are so well known. In fact, only one quarter of the world's deserts are sandy, the remainder being stony or bare rock, but as deserts make up one-fifth of the

Oasis in Sinai. Arabs collecting dates from a palm tree.

world's land surface, there is still a vast expanse of sand.

Sand forms wherever rocks are being weathered, and the particles are then blown by the wind and deposited to form sheets of sand or *sand dunes*. Sand dunes are always moving and changing shape because there is no vegetation to anchor them, but they do tend to occur either in a crescent shape or as an elongated ridge. The crescent dunes are called *barchans* and they initially form round an obstacle such as a bush or a large rock. They may be up to 30 metres in height and up to 1 kilometre in width. The long dunes are called *seifs*, and they sometimes extend for miles, especially in the great Libyan sand desert.

A wind carrying sand has considerable powers of erosion. For example, in Australia the first telegraph poles to be erected were destroyed by the action of wind and sand. Any upstanding rocks in desert areas are eroded by wind-blown sand to a height of 1·5 metres; above this level sand is not blown. The lower parts of rocks are always eroded more quickly than the upper parts and so overhanging rocks result. These are called *mushroom rocks*.

Although rain is infrequent in deserts, there is a little and it normally falls in heavy downpours. As it rushes away over the ground, it transports sand and larger rocks and therefore has considerable powers of erosion. The water carves deep steep-sided valleys called *wadis*. They are steep-sided because there is little rain to make the slopes as gentle as they are in wetter regions. The streams flowing in wadis are intermittent, and flow only for a few days or weeks each year.

There are some permanent rivers which flow through deserts after receiving water from mountains or wet areas outside the desert. The Nile and Colorado are the biggest examples of such rivers. The meandering of the Nile has carved a valley which is wide enough for cultivation, and there are irrigated fields alongside the river. The Colorado has only eroded vertically in parts of its course, carving out canyons such as the Grand Canyon, which is nearly 1900 metres in depth and more than 300 kilometres long. There are many canyons in western U.S.A. and in other deserts throughout the world. The canyons of the United States are acknowledged as the biggest. They are so big because there is an alternating series of hard and soft rocks arranged horizontally and the harder strata protect the softer. Thus, the steep valley walls are preserved.

Water in deserts will often support oases. Examples are the long ribbon-like oases along the Nile, and the Peruvian rivers which cross the Atacama. There are also small oases where underground water can be reached by digging a well, and where a few palm trees grow.

View of the Grand Canyon in Arizona from the south rim.

Limestone

Limestone consists of the remains of dead sea creatures which used calcium carbonate to make up their hard parts. The calcium content of limestone makes it easy to identify, as it will effervesce (or fizz) when a drop of dilute hydrochloric acid is placed on it. Limestone may contain many shells or the remains of coral and is then known as shelly limestone or coralline limestone, respectively.

Carboniferous limestone dates from the Carboniferous period of 300 million years ago. It is a hard rock and forms high ground such as parts of the Pennines, the Mendips, or Dalmatia in Yugoslavia. In Dalmatia a barren limestone area is known as Karst – a name now used to denote all similar limestone regions throughout the world. Karst scenery contains flat limestone outcrops known as *limestone pavements*. The pavements consist of flat slabs or *clints*, separated by enlarged vertical cracks or joints which are known as *grykes*. A gryke enlarged by flowing water could become a pot hole or a swallow hole. A pot hole is a vertical hole large enough for a man to descend, and a swallow hole is a pot hole containing flowing water (which is swallowed). Limestone is permeable as it allows water to pass through the joints. Hence, underground streams occur, and they dissolve the limestone to create caverns in which *stalactites* and *stalagmites* form. If a stalactite grows down to meet a stalagmite it is known as a *rock pillar*. These features come about in the same way –

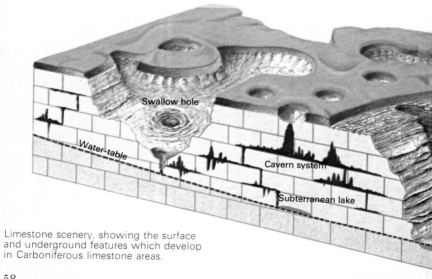

Limestone scenery, showing the surface and underground features which develop in Carboniferous limestone areas.

the calcium in dripping water solidifies to form rock. These new rocks can all be called *dripstones*.

Many buildings and walls in Carboniferous limestone areas are built of the local rock. Another type of limestone, Jurassic or Oolitic limestone, is also used for building. This is softer, but pale yellowish and therefore more attractive, and is sometimes known as Bath stone. Bath and many other towns of western England contain buildings made of this Oolitic limestone. The softest limestone is called chalk, and this is pure calcium carbonate. It is quite porous, meaning that between the grains of rock there are small holes called pores through which water can trickle. Like other limestones, chalk contains many dry valleys which must have been eroded by surface rivers, though the water

has now disappeared underground. Chalk forms hills, as its porosity ensures that water sinks into the rock, rather than eroding it. The hills are rounded and often have a steep slope called an *escarpment* on one side, and a gentle slope or dip on the other side. White outcrops are often clearly seen, either where there are quarries to obtain chalk for making cement, or on coastlines. The white cliffs at Dover in England are particularly impressive. The water passing through chalk often emerges as a spring at the foot of the hill. Many villages are located on these springs as they provide a reliable supply of pure water.

In tropical areas such as Jamaica, limestone areas are very distinctive as the great heat and heavy rainfall combine to promote rapid rock removal.

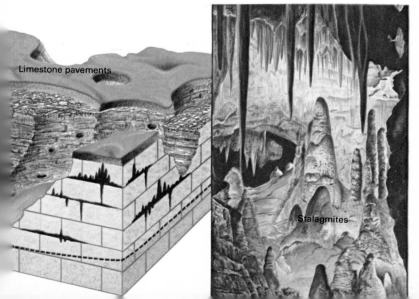

Limestone pavements

Stalagmites

Lakes

Lakes are only temporary features of the landscape because rivers flowing into them deposit silt which will eventually fill the lake and leave a flat fertile plain. There are many old lake beds such as the Vale of Pickering in northern England or parts of the Red River Valley on the Prairies of Canada and U.S.A. Lakes are caused by there being too much water in one area, a high water table, or a hollow which is underlain by impervious rocks.

Lakes may result from the erosion of a hollow, deposition forming a dam, or tectonic activity. Tectonic activity may create large lakes such as Lakes Malawi and Tanganyika or Loch Ness, which are in rift valleys.

Lakes of deposition include man-made lakes behind a dam, and even those dammed by beavers. Loch Lomond has formed behind a moraine, and Ullswater is dammed by glacial till. Many coastal lagoons such as the Fleet at Chesil Beach are dammed by deposition, and deltaic and oxbow lakes are other examples. The Sea of Galilee is dammed by a lava flow.

Lakes of erosion may be associated with corries and ribbon lakes in glaciated areas – for example, Red Tarn and Wastwater in the Lake District – wind-formed hollows in deserts, or man-made hollows as in sand and gravel pits.

Things to do

● Visit the National Geological Museum.
● Visit your local Museum to study the rock collection.

The Kariba dam on the river Zambesi.

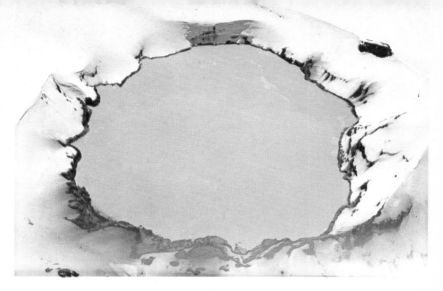

New Zealand. The Tongariro crater lake is over 6500 metres above sea level, hence the snow cover in winter.

● On holiday at the seaside, or in the hills, look at the different rocks and make notes about each specimen describing its appearance and location.

● Look at the soil in a hole or road cutting. Can you see the horizons?

● Look at the hills and valleys in the countryside, and try and explain why they are there.

● See which river features you can identify in your nearest river valley.

● If you visit a glaciated area, see which Ice Age features you can recognize.

● Follow the newspapers for reports on earthquakes and volcanoes. Keep a scrap book of cuttings.

● List the evidence of erosion and deposition when you next visit a coastal area.

● At the beach, can you see which way the longshore drift is moving?

● Which side of a promontory is being eroded more rapidly?

● On sandy beaches, look at the little channels of flowing water as the tide goes out, and you can see miniature examples of meanders and river cliffs.

● Coastal sand dunes will show some desert characteristics. Look at the ripples of sand on the seashore too.

● Limestone and chalk hills can be identified by their characteristic shape.

● When you see a lake, ask yourself how it was formed. What scraped out the hollow, or what made the dam?

Weather and Climate

Climate

The atmosphere extends for thousands of kilometres above the surface of the earth, gradually thinning out into space. There are several layers which show great variations, and they protect the earth from meteorites and the burning heat of the sun.

The composition of the atmosphere is a mixture of gases, 78% being nitrogen and 21% being oxygen, with smaller quantities of other gases such as argon, carbon dioxide and water vapour. There are also particles of dust and dirt, salt, pollen and bacteria. The lower and denser parts of the atmosphere contain most of these including all the water vapour, so the weather changes are restricted to the lower layers. The amount of water vapour changes with evaporation and condensation. The only other change is in the amount of carbon dioxide. The burning of fuels, and variations in vegetation cover cause slight variations. If all the world's forests were removed, the variation would be rather large, however, and might dramatically alter the climatic conditions on earth.

The lowest part of the atmosphere is called the *troposphere*, and extends up to the tropopause. Temperatures in the troposphere decrease upwards at the rate of 1°C for 165 metres. The height of the tropopause varies daily but averages 17 kilometres at the equator and 6 kilometres at the poles.

Above the tropopause is the *stratosphere*, which contains no water vapour and hence no clouds, and has a uniform temperature. Up to about 80 kilometres the composition of the atmosphere remains the same, but at higher levels the oxygen and nitrogen decrease, and

Some meteorological records.

Highest temperatures recorded
(in a Stevenson Screen)
°C
56·6 Death Valley, California, 1913.
58·5 Al Aziziyah, Libya, 1922.

Lowest temperatures recorded
(in a Stevenson Screen)
°C
−68 at Oimyakon, Siberia, 1892.
−68 at Verkhoyansk, Siberia, 1933.
−87 at Vostok, Antarctica, 1960.
−73 at South Pole in Antarctica, 1957.

Heaviest Rainfall
31 mm in 1 minute in Maryland, U.S.A., 1956.
1870 mm in 24 hours in Reunion, Indian Ocean, 1952.
9200 mm in a month at Cherrapunji, Assam, 1861.
26400 mm in a year at Cherrapunji, 1861.

Heaviest Snowfall
25800 mm of snow on Mt Rainier in Washington, U.S.A.

Biggest Hailstones
0·75 kg (18 cm diameter) hailstone in Kansas, 1970.

Heaviest Rainfall in Britain
279 mm in 24 hours in Dorset, 1955.
1422 mm in a month on Snowdon, 1909.
6527 mm in a year at Sprinkling Tarn, 1954.

above 800 kilometres the atmosphere consists mainly of hydrogen and helium, both of which are light gases.

The *ionosphere* contains electrified molecules which have the property of reflecting radio waves, thereby bending them and turning them back down to earth. Without the ionosphere, transmission of radio signals over great distances around the earth would be difficult or impossible. Another important layer is the *ozone layer* situated about 65 kilometres above the surface. Ozone is oxygen with 3 atoms instead of 2 in each molecule. Ozone results from the ultraviolet light in the sun's rays changing ordinary oxygen. The ultra violet rays would be harmful, and possibly lethal, if they reached the earth's surface, but the ozone absorbs them, thus protecting the lower parts of the atmosphere.

The rays of sunlight are travelling from 149 million kilometres away, and when they reach the earth they are parallel rays. The curve of the earth means that although the rays of sunlight may be vertical at the equator, they are at quite a low angle when they reach temperate latitudes. The rays lose heat as they pass through the atmosphere and so, the more direct the journey, the greater the heat which penetrates through to the surface of the earth. The vertical rays in equatorial latitudes cause the tropical regions to be much warmer than the regions

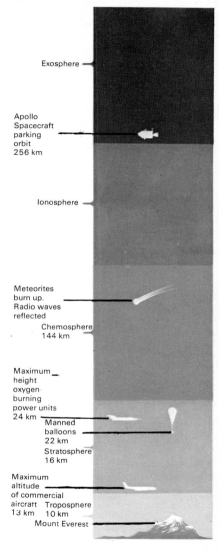

Exosphere

Apollo
Spacecraft
parking
orbit
256 km

Ionosphere

Meteorites
burn up.
Radio waves
reflected
Chemosphere
144 km

Maximum
height
oxygen
burning
power units
24 km
Manned
balloons
22 km
Stratosphere
16 km

Maximum
altitude
of commercial
aircraft   Troposphere
13 km   10 km
Mount Everest

The earth's atmosphere showing the different layers and their heights.

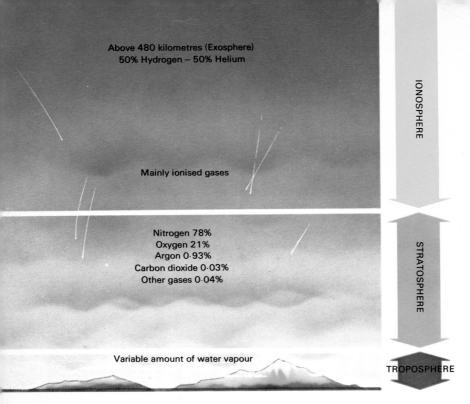

Above 480 kilometres (Exosphere)
50% Hydrogen – 50% Helium

Mainly ionised gases

Nitrogen 78%
Oxygen 21%
Argon 0·93%
Carbon dioxide 0·03%
Other gases 0·04%

Variable amount of water vapour

IONOSPHERE

STRATOSPHERE

TROPOSPHERE

Composition of the atmosphere and the variations with height.

at temperate latitudes. In spite of seasonal changes the equatorial regions always have the mid-day sun at a high angle in the sky. On the equator the lowest mid-day angle of the sun is 66½°, when the overhead sun is 23½° north in June or 23½° south in December. The highest angle of the mid-day sun decreases by 1° of angle, for every degree of latitude the sun has moved away.

Continuous heat at the equator ensures that there is rising air throughout the year. This rising air creates a low pressure region known as the *equatorial low pressure* or *doldrum belt*. The doldrums are noted for calms, but thunderstorms and heavy rainfall are common. The air which rises from the doldrums circulates around the atmosphere; some falls in low latitudes, some travels nearly to the poles before falling, but the main mass falls at about 25° north and 25° south. This falling air gives rise to regions of high pressure which are known as the *tropical highs* or *horse latitudes*.

The falling air near the tropics cannot just disappear, but travels across the surface of the earth. Air moving across the surface is known as wind, and some of the major planetary winds have their source in this falling air. Some air moves from the horse latitudes near the tropic of Cancer towards the doldrum low pressure belt, turning to its right as it travels because of the effects of the rotation of the earth. The resulting winds are the *north-east trades*, which blow from the north-east towards the equator.

All winds are named according to the direction *from* which they blow. Air moves from the horse latitudes near the tropic of Capricorn towards the doldrum low pressure belt, turning to its left as it travels because of the effects of the rotation of the earth. All moving bodies turn to their left in the southern hemis-phere, but to their right in the northern hemisphere. These southern hemisphere winds are called the *south-east trades*. The air from the horse latitudes which moves towards the equator creates the trades, but there is also air moving towards temperate latitudes. The resulting winds are called the *wester-lies*. In the northern hemisphere they flow from the horse latitudes, turn to their right and are *south-westerlies*, whereas in the southern hemisphere they blow from the horse latitudes, turn to their left and are *north-westerlies*. These westerlies are particularly persistent and are called the Roaring Forties.

In addition to the falling air of the tropics there is also falling air in the Arctic and Antarctic, where it is so cold. From these two high pressure areas, winds blow out into temperate latitudes and meet the wester-lies. Where the tropical westerly air meets the cold polar air, friction creates a whirling air mass which will eventually form a *depression*.

The circulation of the world's major winds.

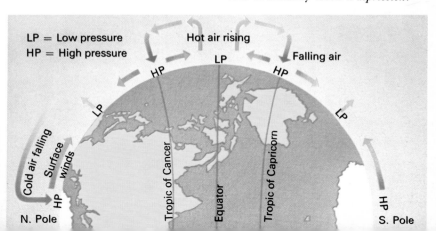

Climatic Factors

The main factors which affect climatic conditions are latitude, land and sea, and altitude, with minor local considerations such as aspect.

Latitude determines the angle of the mid-day sun, and the temperatures generally decrease from the equator towards the pole. However, in summer the tropical regions are actually hotter than the lands on the equator, because the sun is overhead and skies are usually clear, whereas the cloudiness at the equator reduces the amount of sunshine. Latitude also influences rainfall; from 0°–10° north and south is a wet area because of the doldrum belt, whereas 20°–30° is dry because of the horse latitudes.

Land and sea have an effect on both temperature and rainfall. Land heats up and cools down more quickly than the sea. For those who live near the sea, summer heat seems less intense (which is useful in the tropics), and winter temperatures seem much milder (which is advantageous in cooler latitudes). Tropical land masses in summer become hot and develop low pressure systems, thereby attracting winds from the sea. Temperate land masses in winter become very cold and develop high pressure systems, so that dry winds blow out.

There are also land and sea variations in rainfall. Onshore winds are always likely to bring rain so that coastal areas are usually wetter than the interiors. In the equatorial rainfall belt the rain is mostly convectional and is spread fairly evenly across the width of the continent, although coastlines do receive extra rainfall brought by the winds. In temperate latitudes the westerlies

The distribution of average temperatures for July.

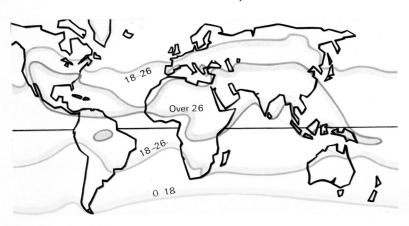

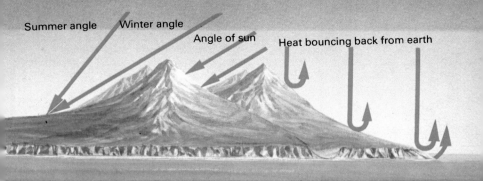

Summer angle   **Winter angle**

Angle of sun

Heat bouncing back from earth

Rays of sunlight bringing heat to the earth.

bring the rainfall; this is heaviest on western coasts and gradually decreases inland. Part of coastal Europe receives 1000–2500 milli-metres, whereas inland, average falls are only 500 millimetres.

Altitude affects the distribution of both rainfall and temperature.

The distribution of average temperatures for January.

Temperatures always decrease with altitude because the air becomes thinner and more rarefied and is unable to retain the heat from the sun. The average rate of tempera-ture decrease is 1°C for every 165 metres. Rainfall also decreases with altitude in the tropics where the type of rainfall is convectional. In temperate latitudes, however, the rainfall (and snow) increases with altitude up to 2–3000 metres where the air becomes too cold to hold much moisture.

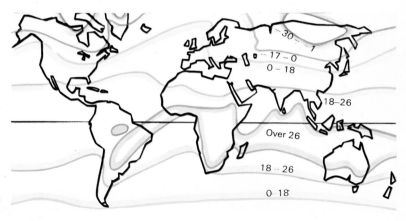

30

17 – 0

0 – 18

18–26

Over 26

18 – 26

0 – 18

Meteorology

Meteorology is the study of weather and *climatology* is the study of climate. Weather is what we experience (or suffer) each day and all the daily weather records, added together and averaged out, will represent the climate. So climate is large scale, general and average, but weather is the minute-by-minute or day-by-day situation. Weather is determined by all the climatic factors already mentioned, and also by the wind direction.

Wind carries masses of air from one place to another, and if the air is coming from a very cold locality, the wind will feel very cold. If the wind is blowing from a damp tropical region, it will bring warm, wet weather. The air masses are named according to their source region. For example, maritime tropical air (mT) comes from a warm tropical ocean, whereas continental tropical (cT) comes from a hot land mass. Other air masses are maritime polar (mP), maritime Arctic or Antarctic (mA), continental polar (cP) and continental Arctic (cA). If continental Arctic blows over Britain in winter it brings bitterly cold Siberian type weather, whereas maritime tropical air would bring very mild, damp conditions. As they travel across ocean or land these air masses gradually change and eventually lose their own characteristics.

Weather Forecasting

Weather forecasting is a form of intelligent guesswork using as much knowledge and information as is available. There is never sufficient information available because of the shortage of weather stations on land and at sea. Also there is little information available for the upper parts of the troposphere. However, we now have much more knowledge and information at our fingertips than we did 10 years ago. The information is studied and analysed, weather maps are drawn, and a forecast is made as quickly as possible. In order to speed up this operation computers are now used by major forecasting centres such as the British Meteorological Office at Bracknell, England. Television,

Major air masses over Australia and New Zealand.

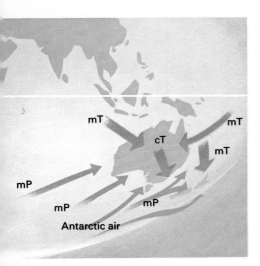

radio and newspaper forecasts are all obtained from this office.

Once the forecast has been made, work will start on the next map so that the forecast can be revised every 2 or 3 hours because weather systems change so quickly. The up-to-date forecasts are generally pressure systems. High pressure systems or *anticyclones* are fairly slow-moving and once they have been established, forecasting is quite easy as changes will be gradual. Low pressure systems or *depressions* move across the surface of the earth at about 40 km/h, but some-

A North Atlantic weather map showing masses of isobars and the existing high and low pressure systems.

very accurate for a short period of time – say, 6 hours – but become less precise for 12 or 24 hours ahead. Forecasts can now be made for the week, and even for the next month, but these are always rather vague and generalized, and they attempt to predict general patterns of weather rather than the precise events.

The commonest patterns of weather are those associated either with low pressure systems or high times suddenly quicken or slow down. They may also change direction slightly – a rain belt expected to pass over southern England, for example, may move north and pass over central Scotland instead. To a meteorologist this is merely a change of direction, but to people living in central Scotland it would seem much worse. Forecasting in Britain is particularly difficult because it is a very small country and weather in the westerly belt is always changing. Most weather comes from the west where there are few weather stations to provide accurate information.

Weather Instruments

Weather stations require information on pressure, temperature, humidity, precipitation, wind and sunshine. The central point of any weather station is the Stevenson Screen which is a white box standing on legs 1–1·5 metres above the ground. It is light-coloured to reflect heat, and it has louvred sides like a perature readings throughout the world.

Pressure can be most accurately recorded by a *mercury barometer*. A column of mercury nearly 75 centimetres high balances the weight of the atmosphere and moves up or down with changes of pressure. Much smaller and more convenient – though slightly less accurate – is

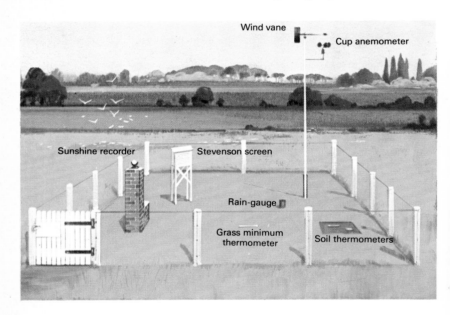

The instruments at a meteorological station.

Venetian blind, to allow air to circulate but to prevent the full force of the wind entering. The shade and shelter of the Stevenson Screen ensures standardisation of all tem-

the *aneroid barometer*. This is a small cylinder with flexible sides from which most of the air has been removed. Changes of air pressure will cause the aneroid to move in and out. By attaching a lever and arm to the aneroid it is possible to make a *barograph*. On the end of the arm is a nib containing slow-drying ink which will last for a week or more. The nib rests on a piece of paper on a revolving drum which is driven by clockwork. As the drum turns round, the nib makes a line which moves up and down with the pressure changes. Each week, a new piece of paper can be attached to the drum in order to obtain a continuous record of pressure changes.

A *thermograph* works in a similar way, writing a continuous record of any temperature changes. The nib moves up or down as a result of the expansion or contraction of two strips of metal at the end of the arm.

Precise temperature records are obtained from thermometers. Maximum and minimum thermometers record the highest temperature during the day and the lowest temperature during the night. A metal rod is pushed along the thermometer by the mercury in the maximum thermometer, and is left at the highest point when the temperature starts to fall. This means the observer can find out the maximum temperature during the previous 24 hours by looking at the thermometer once only, and not every few minutes. The rod can be moved to re-set the thermometer for the next 24 hours. There are also grass minimum thermometers which record the lowest night temperature about 5 centimetres above the ground. Wet and dry bulb thermometers give meteorologists information about relative humidity.

Maximum thermometer

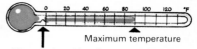

Maximum temperature

Mercury thread breaks at constriction as temperature falls. The thermometer is reset by shaking the mercury back into the bulb.

Minimum thermometer

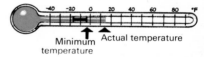

Minimum temperature Actual temperature

Index is drawn back to minimum position as temperature falls. The thermometer is reset by tilting it, bulb end upwards.

Maximum and minimum thermometers.

Rainfall is recorded in a *rain gauge*, a cylindrical tube in which water (and snow) accumulates. The quantity is measured and recorded once each day.

Wind can be recorded by *anemometers*, some of the more expensive models actually keeping a written record of wind speed and direction. Others simply total up the number of revolutions made by the cups, from which an average wind speed may be deduced. Others have a scale which can be read off whenever required.

Sunshine is recorded by a circular magnifying glass which allows the sun's rays to scorch a mark on special paper.

Depression

A depression is an area of low pressure and is sometimes known as a *temperate cyclone*. On a weather map it is shown by a vaguely circular mass of lines with the lowest pressure (970–980 millibars) in the centre, and steadily rising pressure working away from the centre. The lines joining places of equal pressure are called *isobars*, and they are measured in international units known as millibars. Average sea level pressure is about 1000 millibars.

Depressions form where two different air masses pass alongside each other. In the North Atlantic the warm tropical air is heading northwards and the cold Arctic air is travelling southwards. The dividing line between these two air masses is called the *Polar Front*. Friction between these two masses along the Polar Front creates a whirling motion which is followed by an upward movement of air. This in turn draws in more air and so a whirling mass of rising air is created. As it is located in the temperate latitudes where the westerly movement of air occurs, the entire whirling mass of the depression travels from west to east at between 30 and 65 km/h. Depressions have diameters which average about 600 kilometres but can be as much as 3000 kilometres. Within the depressions the winds will be blowing in a variety of directions, being southerly at the leading or eastern edge, and northerly at the rear of the

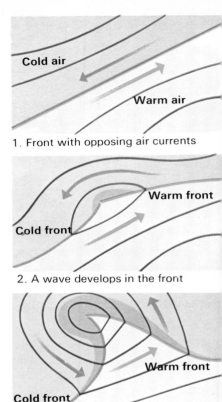

1. Front with opposing air currents

2. A wave develops in the front

3. Fully developed depression

Diagram to show the cold polar air and warm tropical air developing the circulation which becomes a depression.

depression. The depression will contain some cold polar air but also mild tropical air, and the dividing lines between these different air masses are called *fronts*.

A warm front represents the leading edge of a mass of warm air, whilst a cold front is the leading edge of some cold air. Normal depressions contain a warm front which comes first, and a cold front. The air in between the two fronts is called the *warm sector*. As the cold front travels more quickly than the warm front, the two fronts gradually merge to form an occlusion. different types of weather will be experienced. The beginning of the depression will be characterised by high cloud and southerly winds, assuming the centre of the depression to be located to the north. Gradually the cloud cover will become thicker and lower, and

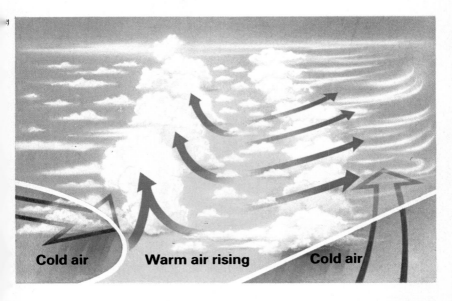

Cold air   Warm air rising   Cold air

The rising air masses associated with the fronts in a depression.

Whenever fronts occur, there are two different masses of air and one mass must be lighter than the other. Therefore, some air will always rise at a front, and as rising air causes rain, fronts will invariably be associated with rainfall.

As a depression passes overhead when the warm front arrives rain will fall. The temperature will rise and the wind will become westerly. In the warm sector the weather will be mild and cloudy and then, when the cold front arrives, heavy rain will fall. The temperature will fall, the wind will become northerly, and the weather will become brighter as the cold front moves away eastwards.

Anticyclone and Ridge

Unlike a depression, which always gives unsettled windy and cloudy weather, the high pressure systems give dry settled periods, often with clear skies and hot sun. An anticyclone is a vaguely circular weather system with high pressure (about 1030 millibars) in the centre decreasing outwards. Winds blow out from the centre in a clockwise direction. Extensions of high pressure bulging out from anticyclones are called *ridges* or *wedges*, and they give similar weather to the main high pressure region.

In the summer months, the northern hemisphere horse latitude region (called the Azores High in the North Atlantic region) moves northwards and may extend over southern England bringing hot sunny weather. The weather associated with this high pressure is similar to typical conditions experienced in the Mediterranean lands throughout the summer, or the Sahara throughout the year. When the settled anticyclonic conditions prevail, dew occurs and there is early morning mist. The morning sunshine soon clears the mist away but in a winter anticyclone, frost and fog would be very slow to clear, and might even persist right through the short winter day. Winter anticyclones may come to the British Isles from the Eurasian land mass. The cold land becomes a region of high pressure from which anticyclones may extend westwards to bring cold conditions to Britain. Fog and smog may develop in these conditions.

Circulation of an anticyclone and anticyclonic conditions – summer and winter.

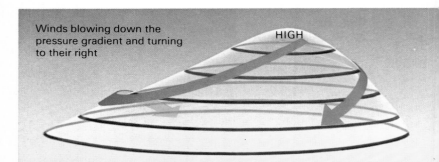

Winds blowing down the pressure gradient and turning to their right

HIGH

Trough, Col and Airstreams

An extension from an anticyclone is called a *ridge*, which suggests something high, while an extension from a depression is called a *trough*, which suggests something low. A trough will often contain a front, normally occluded, and will often bring 1 or 2 hours of heavy rainfall.

If a weather map contains depressions and anticyclones, there is often a gap between two neighbouring anticyclones and two depressions. The area in between them is called a *col*, and containing few or no isobars, is an area of calm. Cols are a very short-lived feature and never survive more than 12 or at most 24 hours, because the movements of depressions will replace them. However, while they are there they will give calm sunny weather in summer with the possibility of thunderstorms and, in winter, unpleasant foggy and possibly freezing conditions.

The outer fringes of an anticyclone may be the same area as the outer fringes of a depression, and in these regions, mid-way between high and low pressure, the isobars often run parallel to each other. These areas of parallel isobars are called *airstreams*.

Winds should blow from high pressure to low pressure but are deflected and end up blowing almost parallel to the isobars. These airstreams can bring very varied weather. An easterly airstream in winter blowing from Europe to Britain would bring sub-zero temperatures and might pick up moisture crossing the North Sea to give some snowfalls near the east coast. South-westerly airstreams always bring mild but damp weather.

Weather map showing a col and two airstreams.

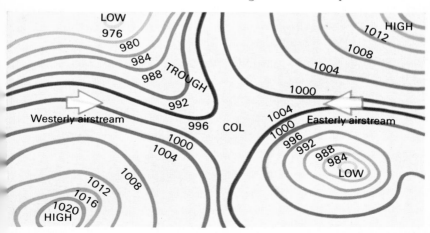

75

Hurricanes

Hurricanes are called *tropical cyclones* in the Indian Ocean, *typhoons* in the China Sea, and *willy-willies* in Australia. They are all whirling masses of air and are like very deep, intense depressions.

The great heat and moisture of the tropics gives the hurricanes their energy and causes rapid uplift and strong winds. The average hurricane has a diameter of about 400 kilometres and travels at about 20 km/h. They all move from east to west because of the general movement of the air in the tropics. In the northern hemisphere they turn to

The location of hurricanes and a diagram to show the whirling mass of air and the calm centre (eye) of a hurricane.

and a southerly one at the back (eastern). In the southern hemisphere those directions are reversed. Wind speeds invariably exceed 150 km/h and often reach 300 km/h. Winds of this speed cause rough seas which damage coastlines, and they also destroy crops such as sugar cane or bananas, causing much suffering to farmers. There are generally 8 to 10 hurricanes per annum in the Caribbean area, and each one is given a girl's name. The first of the season has a name beginning with A, the second with B, and so on. The season for hurricanes is the late summer when there is most heat available. There are often as many as 30 a year in the Pacific Ocean and they often uproot trees and destroy flimsy houses.

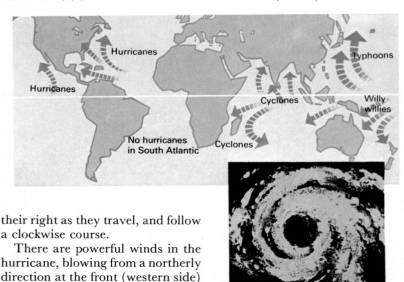

their right as they travel, and follow a clockwise course.

There are powerful winds in the hurricane, blowing from a northerly direction at the front (western side)

Tornadoes

Hurricanes are small, compressed and intensified depressions. If a hurricane is compressed still further, a tornado results. A tornado is a very small whirling mass of air containing the wind and energy of a depression. An average tornado only covers 200–300 metres and moves across country at about 40 km/h. The winds inside the tornado exceed 200 km/h and speeds up to 500 km/h have been recorded. A typical tornado will last for less than an hour but can cause complete devastation in a small area. Buildings often collapse outwards because the pressure inside is higher than that outside with the arrival of the tornado, and then the roofs will fall in. So, it is much safer to be out-of-doors in a tornado than inside a flimsy house. The Mississippi Basin of the U.S.A. suffers from more tornadoes than any other part of the world, and many of the houses contain cellars where the inhabitants shelter when a tornado is forecast.

Tornadoes form in hot land areas, especially in late summer. Hot air rises rapidly and draws in winds to the central funnel. This central area sucks up dust which gives the funnel its characteristic dark colour, and it has also been known to lift small animals. Tornadoes are known as 'twisters' in the U.S.A., and they occur in large numbers because of the great heat of the land and the vast expanse of flat land in the centre of the continent. There are well over 100 tornadoes every year in central U.S.A. Small tornadoes, or dust devils, occur in many countries, and occasionally there is one in Britain (e.g. in Northamptonshire in January, 1975.)

When tornadoes pass over water, they turn into waterspouts. Waterspouts cause less damage because they can be seen and avoiding action taken.

The dark funnel of a tornado; a water spout; the dust caused by the powerful winds of tornadoes.

Thunder and Lightning

Thunder and lightning occur in thunderstorms, which are storms associated with the rapid uplift of air resulting from great heat. The hot air rises very quickly and, as it does so, the air cools and raindrops form. If the raindrops become too large they will subsequently split and give off small charges of electricity. Positive and negative charges accumulate in different parts of a cloud and build up to give a powerful flash of electricity, which we call lightning.

The lightning disturbs the air and makes it reverberate with a loud bang which we call thunder. The thunder and lightning occur almost together, but we see the flash first and hear the thunder later. This is because light travels faster than sound. The time gap between seeing and hearing will give some indication of how far away the lightning is. Lightning can strike the same place twice, and large buildings such as the Empire State Building are frequently hit. They have lightning conductors which carry away the electricity to the ground so that it can do no harm. Trees can also attract lightning so it is dangerous to shelter under or near them in a thunderstorm. If lightning could be controlled and used for energy, many of our power problems could be solved.

There is a separation of electrical charge in the clouds.

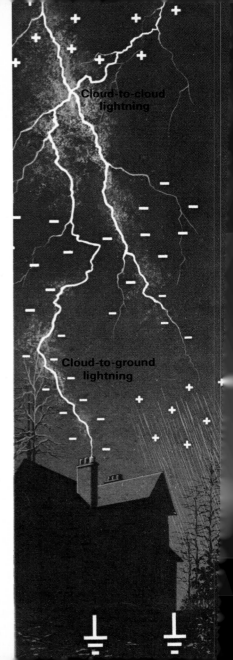

Cloud-to-cloud lightning

Cloud-to-ground lightning

Rain

Rainfall is caused by drops of water vapour, which are present in all air, condensing and becoming visible. These drops are very small, but if several join together they will become heavy enough to fall as one raindrop. If they are too small and light to fall they float in the air as mist or cloud.

The condensation which forms rain is a result of cooling, and the most rapid form of cooling occurs when air rises. There are three main causes of rising air, and hence three types of rainfall. These are *cyclonic*, *convection* and *relief*. Cyclonic rainfall is associated with depressions which are areas of low pressure. Low pressure regions always contain rising air, which causes cooling, condensation and the possibility of rain. Convection rainfall is associated with convection currents caused by hot air rising. The rising air is cooled and hence condensation takes place. The third type of rainfall is orographic or relief rainfall. As winds are forced to rise to pass over mountains, the air cools and condensation occurs. This is why mountainous areas are often cloudy or misty, when surrounding lowlands are bright and sunny. The wettest areas in the world are in mountains such as the Himalayan foothills, Hawaiian highlands, and the coastal hills of Alaska, southern Chile and western Scotland.

Clouds over the Himalayan mountains in Pakistan.

Snow and Hail

If the air temperature falls below freezing point, the drops of water vapour may be turned into tiny ice crystals, and when several ice crystals join together they form a snowflake. Snow is frozen water vapour, not frozen rain.

When snowflakes become heavy enough to fall they descend slowly to the earth, though they often melt and turn into sleet or rain before reaching the ground. Snowfalls are common in many mountainous areas, and also in cold lowland areas in winter. The coldest lands such as the interior of Canada and Siberia do not receive heavy snowfalls because the temperature of the air is too low for it to hold much water vapour. 10 centimetres of snow equal 1 cm of rainfall in water content. When snow is wetter than average, snow ploughs are required to clear it away; drier snow can be removed by snowblowers.

Hail is frozen rain. If a drop of water is carried upwards rapidly, as in a convection current, it may rise so high that it freezes. It then starts to fall, and as it passes through the cloud it gathers more water. If it is carried up again by another rush of air, a second layer of ice will be formed before the small hailstone begins to fall. This process will be repeated several times in the formation of large hailstones. Hailstones may grow as large as golf balls in tropical convection currents, and may weigh $0 \cdot 5$ kg.

Snowstorm affecting people and vehicles in New York City.

Dew and Frost

Warm air is able to hold more water vapour than cold air, and so when air becomes cooler – after sunset, for example – the air may become so cool that it has to deposit some of its moisture. If this moisture condenses in the air it is called *mist*, but if it condenses on the ground it is *dew*. Dew is most likely to occur in a calm, settled night after a warm day. The lack of wind is very important, as too much wind will mix different layers of air together and prevent dew (and mist) from forming.

As the air becomes saturated, water droplets are deposited on the ground, but if the temperature falls below freezing point the dew will turn into frost. This type of frost is called *hoar frost*. A second type is *rime frost* which is less common. This forms when drops of water vapour in the air are cooled to below freezing point, but do not actually turn to ice. These are called supercooled droplets and will only form in conditions of calm or very light winds. If an object, such as an aircraft, passes through the supercooled droplets they freeze, and the object is coated with a layer of ice. Light winds carry these supercooled drops onto posts or buildings which receive a feathery coating of ice crystals on the windward side. Meteorologists refer to ground frost, which is hoar frost on the surface of the earth, and air frost which means that the air temperature is below zero.

Cloud

Clouds are formed by water droplets condensing; millions of drops are required to form even a small cloud. There are four main groups of cloud: *cumulus, nimbus, stratus* and *cirrus*.

The first three consist chiefly of water droplets, but cirrus clouds consist of ice crystals and are thin, wispy clouds which occur at great altitudes and which give no rain.

Water vapour content of air at various relative humidities.

	Water vapour content – grams per cubic metre				
	51·2	30·4	17·3	9·4	4·9
40°C	100%	59%	34%	18%	10%
30°C		100%	57%	31%	16%
20°C			100%	54%	28%
10°C				100%	52%
0°C					100%

Stratus clouds are sheets of cloud with great horizontal extent. They may be thin and light grey in colour, giving little or no rain, or may be thick and dark grey giving prolonged, steady rain. Cumulus and nimbus clouds both extend vertically, often to great heights. The tallest of these will occur in thunderstorms when there are powerful convection currents, but quite large cumulonimbus clouds may occur at warm or cold fronts in depressions. Cumulus are white fluffy clouds which look like pieces of cotton wool. The larger they are, the darker they become because of the water droplets, and they may turn into cumulo-nimbus and bring heavy rain. In addition to the cumulo-nimbus, there are other hybrid versions of clouds called by combinations of the four names already quoted above, e.g. strato-cumulus. The word 'alto' may also be used to indicate high-level clouds, e.g. alto-cumulus. Drops of water only condense on nuclei such as dust or salt. Using this principle attempts have been made to create bigger clouds – and hence make rain – by seeding existing clouds with silver iodide crystals which are good nuclei.

Fog and Mist

Fog and mist are both formed in the same way, as they consist of millions of tiny droplets of floating vapour in the air. These droplets are caused by the condensation of water resulting from the cooling of the air which leads to saturation. The difference between fog and mist is simply one of density. If the visibility is less than one kilometre it is called fog, but if greater than one kilometre it is

Clouds associated with warm and cold fronts.

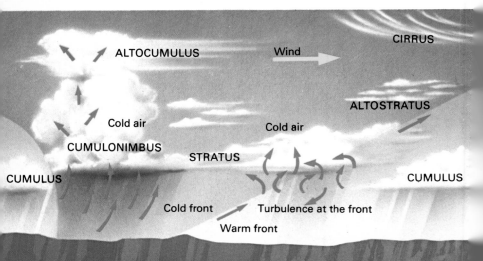

CIRRUS

ALTOCUMULUS   Wind

ALTOSTRATUS

Cold air   Cold air

CUMULONIMBUS   STRATUS

CUMULUS   CUMULUS

Cold front   Turbulence at the front

Warm front

called mist. Fog (or mist) may result from cooling at night; as the ground loses heat after sunset it cools the air above which then becomes saturated. This is called *radiation fog*. Another type is called *advection fog* and results from two air masses meeting and mixing, as happens off Newfoundland where the warm air over the North Atlantic Drift meets the cold air over the Labrador Current.

Fogs can create serious shipping problems and the Newfoundland area has the added danger that icebergs occasionally drift through the region. The U.S. coastguard patrol now warns shipping of such dangers. Fogs also occur over the cool waters of the California and Humboldt Current, and drift on to the neighbouring land. The famous Golden Gate bridge at San Francisco is often mist-covered as a result, and the mists of Chile and Peru are so frequent that they actually provide enough moisture to allow trees to grow on some west-

Different types of fog and some visible effects.

facing slopes on the edges of the Atacama desert.

Fogs occurring over land can create serious travel problems. Visibility may be so poor that airports are closed to reduce the risk of crashes, and there have been instances of sections of motorways being closed because of multiple crashes in foggy conditions.

Fog in industrial areas may collect large numbers of particles of dust and grime. The combination of smoke and fog is called 'smog', and is harmful to lungs.

Things to do

- Look at the angle of the sun at mid-day.
- Which is the sunny side of your house?
- Watch the weather forecast on television or read it in the paper.
- Look at the cloud types each morning.
- Keep a weather diary.
- Keep a diary of disasters (climate and physical).
- Have a close look at the next snowflake you see.

Radiation fog

Sea mist

Freezing fog

The Living World of the Earth

Climate and Vegetation Zones

Climates are often referred to as hot and wet, or mild and damp, but these words are not very precise. Actual temperature and rainfall figures will be used in this chapter to show exactly what is meant by these vague words. Tropical, sub-tropical and temperate climates are also slightly confusing. Tropical climates are really those within the

The chief climate and vegetation zones of the world.

tropics – that is, between 23½° north and 23½°. south. Temperate climates are those which never experience excessive heat. In between the temperate and tropical regions are areas such as parts of India and the Mediterranean lands where summers can be very hot. These lands are called sub-tropical.

The map shows a simplified and generalised division of the world into climatic and vegetation regions. It is very difficult to decide where a forest ends and grassland begins, as there may be many kilometres of grassland with scattered trees in between the true forest and the true grassland. A similar problem applies to locating the edge of the desert. Boundary lines have been drawn for clarity on the map,

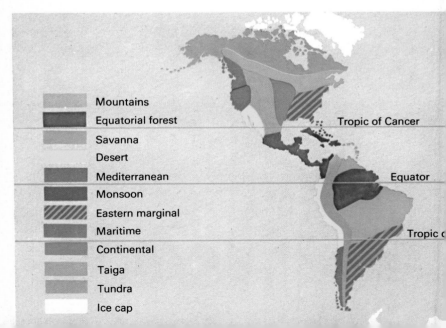

Mountains
Equatorial forest
Savanna
Desert
Mediterranean
Monsoon
Eastern marginal
Maritime
Continental
Taiga
Tundra
Ice cap

Tropic of Cancer

Equator

Tropic o

but they really are zones of transition and not sharp dividing lines.

The equatorial forest region receives rain throughout the year and this is why trees grow. To the north and south of these equatorial forests are the lands which receive rainfall for only part of the year, in the summer months, and here trees do not survive. Grass is the main vegetation, so this land is called savanna or tropical grassland. Moving further from the equator are high pressure belts which bring dry weather and cause the deserts.

Outside the tropics the climatic regions are the Mediterranean, maritime, continental, taiga, tundra and ice cap. Both within tropical latitudes and in temperate lands are the monsoon and mountain climates. Monsoons occur on the eastern sides of continents in all latitudes from 0°–60° north and 0°–40° south, and mountain climates occur wherever a large mountain range is high enough to cause climatic variations.

Mediterranean lands are like deserts in summer, and maritime regions in winter, with thorny scrub and grass. Maritime regions are wet all the year round and so forests can survive. The continental regions have only sufficient rainfall for grassland, and here are found the main temperate grasslands of the northern hemisphere. Taiga and tundra are cold forms of continental, and support coniferous forest and poor Arctic type vegetation, respectively.

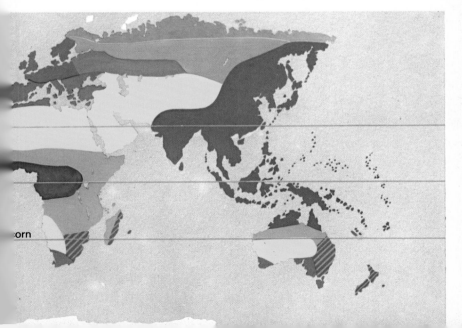

orn

Equatorial Forest

Equatorial forest regions are situated on or near the equator between 5° north and 5° south. They include the Amazon Basin, Zaire Basin and other smaller areas, especially in south-east Asia.

In March or September, when the sun is overhead, the monthly average temperature is about 27°C. When the sun moves away to the tropic of Cancer in June, or tropic of Capricorn in December, these latitudes still receive much heat and average 24°C or 25°C. There is very little change from one month to another because the sun is always high in the sky. The greatest difference is between day and night, and it is sometimes said that night is the winter of the tropics. Daytime temperatures will exceed 30°C while at night the thermometer can fall to

15°C and everyone feels very cold.

Rain falls throughout the year, and there is very little change from one month to another. There is no dry season, but there are often periods of lower rainfall called the drier season. The rain is brought by the doldrums belt and when this moves away, following the sun, the forest regions receive slightly less rainfall.

Every day is hot and wet, and relative humidity is high – over 80%. On many days there is a distinct sequence of weather which, day after day, becomes very monotonous. The morning will be sunny and, as the hot air rises, convection currents form clouds. The clouds become larger during the afternoon until eventually there is a tropical downpour. After this the sky clears just before nightfall. Daylight lasts from 6 a.m. to 6 p.m. on the equator, and there is only a very short time between daylight and complete darkness. Twilight does

The location of the world's chief equatorial forest regions.

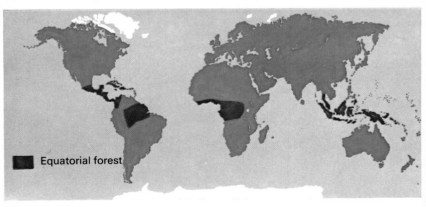

Equatorial forest

A rubber tapper cutting the tree to allow latex to escape.

only reaches 3–4 metres, and above these are small trees which grow to 10–15 metres. In gaps through the foliage of these small trees, other trees grow up to 25 metres, and above these are the giants which reach 40 metres. Viewed from the air, the forests make a carpet of green through which no sunlight and little daylight reach the ground. The only places where undergrowth occurs are where sunlight penetrates, as alongside rivers and in clearings. True jungle is more common in areas with less dense forest, such as in the monsoon lands, or on the edges of the equatorial forests where the tree growth thins out.

There are millions of insects living on the ground in amongst the fallen leaves and rotting vegetation, but larger animals mostly live above the forest floor. Snakes, birds and monkeys are all common tree dwellers.

not occur because the sun sinks below the horizon very quickly.

The daily heat and moisture cause rapid growth of vegetation. The whole area is forested with an enormous range of trees. Most of the trees are deciduous, which means that they shed their leaves. Unlike the deciduous trees in Britain and other temperate countries, where all the leaves fall together in autumn, there are no real seasons in the equatorial forests. A tree will be growing new leaves and shedding old ones every month, so although it is called a deciduous tree, it appears to be evergreen.

The vegetation grows in a series of layers. The lowest layer of shrubs

Monthly temperature and rainfall figures at Manaus, Brazil.

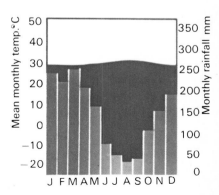

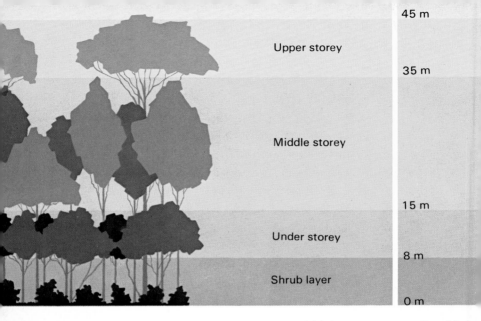

45 m

Upper storey

35 m

Middle storey

15 m

Under storey

8 m

Shrub layer

0 m

Layers of vegetation and their approximate heights above the ground.

Life is not easy in the equatorial forest, although the heat and moisture make growth rapid. Primitive inhabitants were mainly shifting cultivators or hunters and gatherers. The shifting cultivators lived by slash and burn operations, in which they cut down (slashed) and burned trees to make a clearing in which they planted crops such as manioc, yams or sweet potatoes. These crops provided the main source of food.

Each clearing would be used for three or four crops and then abandoned, because the soil would be exhausted. The soils are not very fertile in spite of the luxuriant forests which grow on them. Heavy rain and high temperatures 'leach' the soils, dissolving and removing from them all the chemicals which are essential to plant growth. The dying trees replace these chemicals, but once the trees have been cut down, leaching quickly damages the soil.

Hunters and gatherers such as pygmies hunted for birds and animals, fished the rivers and gathered berries and fruits in order to find enough food. They were nomadic, moving on as soon as they used up the food in one place. They built only temporary shelters of leaves when they were on their travels.

When Europeans moved into the equatorial forest areas they developed plantations, in order to earn money by exporting useful commodities. Rubber, sugar cane, cocoa and bananas can all be grown on plantations in equatorial forest regions, as they require high temperatures and regular rainfall for their growth. The plantations generally used local native labour because it was cheap, and European overseers organised the work. Nowadays, most of the tropical countries operate their own plantations.

Another way in which equatorial forests have been exploited for their wealth is by mining for minerals, such as tin from Malaysia. Once again, Europeans organised the work, using cheap local labour, but now most of the mining in tropical Brazil or Zaire is run by the local people for their own profit.

Many more minerals will doubtless be discovered in these sparsely populated and under-developed forests, but it has not been easy to settle in these areas because of the heat, humidity, and presence of diseases which have been difficult to overcome. Many of these diseases can now be controlled by modern drugs. Even in the Panama Canal Zone many lives were lost during the construction of the canal because of malaria, yellow fever and other diseases. By means of strict regulations most diseases have been brought under control. This shows what can be done, but it has never been easy for white people to lead a successful and energetic life in the equatorial forests.

In the future the countries will develop their own resources steadily, possibly with aid and advice from North American or European countries. It is hoped that, gradually, annual income will increase, as these formerly backward parts of the world improve their living standards.

Mangrove forests occur along the coasts of equatorial forest regions.

Savanna

Savanna regions are located on either side of the equatorial forests, mostly between 5° and 20° north and south of the equator. They occur on the Brazilian Plateau and in the Llanos of Venezuela; in parts of Nigeria and Ghana and southern Zaire and Rhodesia; and in northern Australia. They also occur in Kenya, Uganda and Tanzania, even on the equator, as there is no equatorial forest in eastern Africa. This is because the land is a plateau and the elevation causes lower temperatures and lower rainfall, which prevent forest growth.

Savannas in the northern hemisphere, such as the Llanos, or in Nigeria, have their summer season from May to September, and their winter from November to February. The southern hemisphere savannas

The world's chief savanna regions.

have summer from November to February and winter from May to September. In June, the sun's apparent migration takes it to the tropic of Cancer, and so the northern savannas experience the overhead sun, and temperatures average 25°C or even higher. By December the sun has moved to the tropic of Capricorn and the northern savannas will average about 15°C during these winter months. The southern savannas will also average 25°C in their summer (December) and 15°C in their winter (June).

Rainfall is also affected by the movements of the sun as the doldrums low pressure belt, with its convection rainfall, migrates north in June and then southwards until December. High summer temperatures are accompanied by convection rainfall which will vary from place to place. On the edges of the forest the rain may reach 1250 millimetres, but on the desert margins

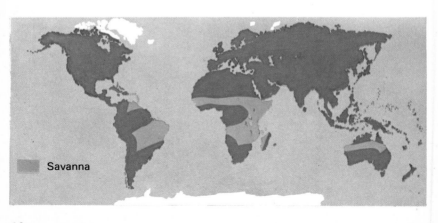

Savanna

will be only 250 mm. In the summer months the savannas are affected by the doldrums and experience conditions similar to those of the equatorial forests. In winter the horse latitudes move in to control climate, and desert-like conditions then prevail.

The seasonal change from hot, wet summers to warm, dry winters creates difficulties for some types of vegetation. If they haven't devised methods of storing water, they shrivel up during the period of drought. The main type of vegetation is grassland which may grow to more than a metre in height during the summer. In the winter it turns brown and shrivels up, to give a very parched appearance. There are also trees, which are very numerous near the edges of the equatorial forest, but non-existent on the desert margins. Some, such as the bottle tree or baobab, can store water inside the trunk, whilst others have small leaves to reduce the water losses. Many trees and bushes are very thorny.

Animals also have to survive the dry season. Some do this by migrating to the forest margin, while others congregate near water holes. Lions, giraffes, zebras and many types of deer are typical of the savannas.

The old primitive ways of life have gradually been disappearing, but traditionally, the natives were either cultivators or herders. The cultivators, such as the Kikuyu in Kenya, had permanent villages around which they grew their crops. The herders, such as the Masai (Kenya and Tanzania), reared large numbers of cattle, generally rather thin beasts, as quantity rather than quality was important for status within the tribe.

Outside influences have led to change in these old ways of life. In Africa many farms were created by Europeans, although they have now largely been taken over by the locals. Coffee was an important cash crop in Kenya, and tobacco in Rhodesia. Better quality cattle have been introduced, though disease carried by the tsetse fly is a serious hindrance.

The savanna region of the Orinoco Basin is called the Llanos and has been a cattle herding region for more than a century. Irrigation schemes are now being developed, as this is the only way to ensure

Monthly temperature and rainfall figures at Ciudad Bolivar, Venezuela.

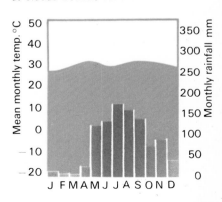

Horses grazing on savannas near Addis
Ababa in Ethiopia.

water supplies during the winter
season. The other savanna region of
South America is in Brazil and is
called Campos. Rich volcanic soils
have helped the growth of coffee for
which Brazil is famous. Cotton,
sugar, oranges, maize and other
crops are all grown, and cattle are
reared. The presence of iron and
other minerals has helped industrial
development. There are some elevated savanna regions in the Andes
of Colombia and Ecuador, and
many more in Central America. In
these regions coffee is the most
important cash crop and maize is
the staple foodstuff.

Australian savannas are mainly
in the Northern Territory and
Queensland, and like most of the
world's tropical grasslands are
sparsely populated. There are some

mineral deposits such as copper at
Cloncurry, which have given rise to
isolated settlements, but most of the
area is used for extensive farming –
that is, rearing a small number of
animals per square kilometre. This
is because the pasture is insufficient
to support larger numbers. Cattle
and sheep are found in these areas,
cattle being more numerous as they
are better able to withstand the
great heat. Water supplies are provided by artesian wells. These are
fed by rain which falls on the Great
Dividing Ranges and travels slowly
underground in an aquifer. A well in
the interior is therefore using water
which has fallen as rain several
hundred kilometres away.

There are tropical grassland
areas in India, but these are part of
the monsoonal area and so the real
savannas only occur in South
America, Africa and Australia.
They cover large areas and are gen-

erally underdeveloped. The vast expanses of grassland would become more productive if regular supplies of water could be provided. If the heavy summer rain, which generally runs away, could be stored for winter use, much more food could be produced.

Dams have been constructed in parts of South American savannas and in Africa. An outstanding area is the Gezira, which is a triangular region between the Blue Nile and White Nile in Sudan. The Sennar Dam regulates the river flow, and guarantees water throughout the year. High quality cotton and food crops are grown. Other large schemes are at Lake Volta in Ghana and Lake Kariba on the Rhodesia-Zambia border. Both of these provide regular water supplies for irri-

gation. The canals from the Volta have unfortunately contributed to the spread of bilharzia, a blood and bladder disease which can be fatal. Bilharzia is caused by a flat worm parasite carried by snails which breed in the irrigation canals.

A large irrigation scheme in Australia is situated along the river Ord in the northern part of Western Australia. This scheme, like all savanna developments, suffers from lack of communications. There are few surfaced roads and few railway lines available. These need money, and people, and savanna areas are short of both of these.

Useful sources of income now being developed, especially in African savannas, are the wild life parks. The abundance of interesting animals encourages tourists, and special areas are now being set aside for the wild animals – for example, the Serengeti Plains in Tanzania.

Australian grassland scene with modern day cowboy.

Deserts

Deserts are located between 20° and 30° north and south in the tropical high pressure belt. They do not normally extend to eastern coasts of land masses because in those areas there are monsoon climates. In the middle of the large continents – chiefly in Asia but also in North America – the deserts extend further north than 30° because their inland location prevents rainfall reaching them either from the west or east coasts. The main locations are the Sahara and Kalahari in Africa; the Atacama in South America; the Navaho, Painted, Sonora and others in North America; the Arabian and Gobi in Asia; and the Western Australian desert.

Summer temperatures are high in these deserts, even in the cool deserts such as the Gobi. The over-head sun and the heating of land masses gives temperatures of 30°C. In winter when the sun moves to the other hemisphere, temperatures fall to 15°C in the main horse latitude deserts such as the Sahara, and to freezing point in parts of the Gobi. On the western margins of the Atacama, the Sahara, the Kalahari and the Western Australian deserts the cool offshore currents – the Humboldt, Canary, Benguela and West Australian respectively – affect the temperatures. Summers are only 15–20°C because of the cooling effects of the sea, but the winter temperatures may be similar to those inland, as the sea temperature does not fall as much as that of the land, and is no longer a cooling influence.

The clear skies of deserts contribute to high daytime temperatures, but also cause a rapid fall with darkness. All the heat radiates up from the land during the night and temperatures will be low, possibly

The location of the world's desert and semi-desert regions.

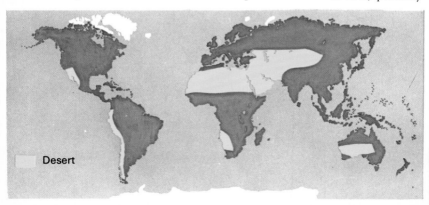

Desert

94

American desert. Navajo Indian land in Arizona.

even falling to freezing point in the Sahara. Because of this great diurnal range, the desert Arabs wear flowing garments which are cool during the day, but provide warmth during the night.

Deserts are noted for their lack of rainfall, and the annual total will be less than 250 mm. The marine deserts are the driest because of the influence of the cool current offshore. Winds blowing from the sea are cooled by the current so that when they reach land they become warmer and will therefore pick up moisture, and certainly not release any. Much of the Atacama receives less than 50 mm per annum.

The rainfall in deserts is not only small in amount, but also unreliable and irregular. Rainstorms are very heavy, and one or two convection thunderstorms may provide the total rainfall for the year. The heavy fall causes rapid floods and the water runs off very quickly, carrying sand and rock fragments, so becoming an active agent of erosion. Narrow steep-sided river channels called *wadis* are formed by the intermittent rivers which flow. Travellers have been known to be caught in wadis down which floods have rushed as the result of rainstorms several kilometres away.

Deserts do contain sand dunes

Monthly temperature and rainfall figures at Timbukto, Mali.

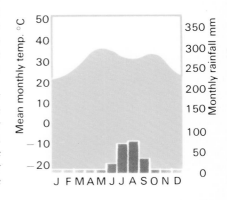

Robed Algerian with camels in the Sahara Desert.

but more frequently they are rocky and stony. There is little vegetation, but few areas are totally devoid. Small spiny bushes have the ability to survive many months without rainfall, and there may also be tufts of coarse grass. Many flowers spring up after rain has fallen, and sometimes completely cover the ground. They quickly go through their life cycle, die off, and leave seeds to wait for the next rain. At oases, the vegetation, notably palm trees, is often luxuriant.

The oases provide locations for permanent settlements, so crops are grown. Those oases which consist of palm trees and a few small fields cluster around a well, but there are larger ribbon-like oases which run along river valleys such as the Nile or the 50 rivers which cross the Atacama in Peru. The palm trees yield dates, but cotton, sugar cane and maize can be grown.

The only permanent desert settlements not situated at oases are those associated with mineral deposits. Money from mining has encouraged the building of towns even when no local water has been available. Several towns in the Atacama of northern Chile receive water piped from the melting snow of the Andes, and Kalgoorlie in Western Australia has water piped from a reservoir near Perth. Kalgoorlie was created because of gold deposits discovered in the late nineteenth century, and on some days there was more gold than water available. Other important mineral deposits in deserts include the diamonds of Kimberley in South Africa, iron at Fort Gouraud in Mauretania and the Hamersley Region in Western Australia, silver and copper in Arizona, and the oil and natural gas deposits of the Saharan and Arabian deserts.

There are still a few nomads living in the deserts, although they have diminished in numbers because outside influences have encouraged them to change their old ways, or have accidentally introduced new and fatal diseases. The Aborigines in Australia, the Bushmen in the Kalahari, and Arab groups such as Bedouin in the Sahara are all well-known desert inhabitants. Life is very difficult for these nomads and although considered very primitive, they have become very efficient and successful at surviving in such a difficult environment. The Aborigines live in primitive shelters and eat almost anything which grows or moves. They successfully hunt animals and have developed the famous boomerang. They also use the woomera, or throwing stick, which enables them to throw spears much greater distances. The woomera has given its name to the Australian-British rocket range in South Australia, which tests rockets by firing them into the desert.

The Bushmen also eat anything they can find, and have evolved a successful mode of survival in the Kalahari. The Sahara contains the most advanced group of ancient settlers, and some of these Arabs were herders of animals, not merely hunters and gatherers. Much of their success was due to the camel. This animal has the ability to survive without water for several days, large feet which prevent it from sinking into sand, and double eyelids to protect its eyes from sandstorms. Camel flesh and milk will provide food and drink as well.

Aborigines in corroboree with didgeridoos and spears.

Mediterranean

The Mediterranean regions are mainly located between 30° and 40° north and south on the western sides of continents. They occur all around the Mediterranean Sea and also in California, central Chile, near Cape Town in South Africa, and around Perth and Adelaide in Australia.

Summer temperatures are high, 20–25°C, as the tropical horse latitudes move with the sun to bring desert conditions to the Mediterranean lands. In California and around the Mediterranean Sea, the summer season is May to September, whereas in Chile, South Africa and Australia it is November to March. In the winter, mild maritime conditions move to these regions and temperatures are about 10°C, although there is still ample sunshine.

The location of the world's chief Mediterranean regions.

The winter is the rainy season, as only isolated thunderstorms occur in the summer. In winter there are depressions travelling from west to east in Mediterranean regions, and so coastal areas and west-facing hills are much wetter than inland, sheltered locations. Mountains may receive over 1000 mm, coastal lowlands about 750 mm, and interior locations as little as 350 mm per annum.

The hot, dry summers and mild, wet winters give rise to Mediterranean vegetation which has to be drought-resistant. Trees grow in the wettest areas, and grassland occurs, but most typical is the thorny and aromatic scrub known as *maquis* in southern Europe, *chaparral* in California and *mallee* in Australia. The bushes have spines, or waxy leaves or thick bark in order to help survive the summer drought, and include laurel and lavender. The cork oak has developed its thick bark in order to prevent loss of mois-

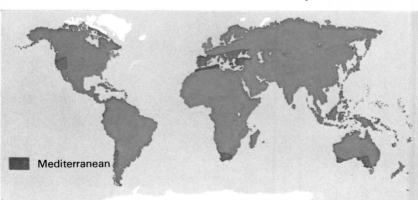

Mediterranean

The Parthenon – the ruined remains of Athena's temple, near Athens.

ture in the hot dry months.

There are many differences between the lands around the Mediterranean Sea and the other Mediterranean regions, because of the length of settlement. The ancient civilizations of Greece and Rome flourished in these excellent climatic conditions long before settlement occurred in California or Australia.

The climatic conditions are suitable for certain types of farming, for example, cereals which will grow during the mild, wet winters and will ripen in the hot, dry summers. Similarly, fruit will also ripen well, and can be dried in the sun to make prunes, currants, raisins and so on. Farming in southern Europe and north Africa has tended to follow traditional lines, and small-scale peasant-style farming occurs. Even so, large surpluses of grapes and wine, oranges and olives are exported. Machinery is being introduced to make the farming more efficient and irrigation schemes are being developed.

California, South Africa and Australia have no old-style farming but have much successful commercial farming, and wine, fruits and cereals are exported. California utilised the climate in another way – the creation of the film industry at Hollywood. With its reliable summer sunshine the place was ideal for filming.

Monthly temperature and rainfall figures at Algiers, Algeria.

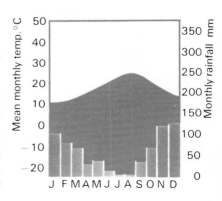

Monsoon and Eastern Marginal

The monsoon lands are located on the eastern sides of the continents between 60° north and 40° south. They extend from Siberia, through China to Malaysia, Burma and India, and via the Indonesian islands to north-east Australia. They also occur on the east coast of Africa from Ethiopia to Natal, in eastern U.S.A. and Canada, and eastern Brazil, Uruguay and Argentina.

The word 'monsoon' does not mean heavy rainfall, but is derived from an Arab word for seasons. Monsoon climates are those which have a seasonal change of wind direction and hence a seasonal change of weather. In the summer months the land masses become hotter than the neighbouring oceans. Therefore low pressure develops over the land with higher pressure over the sea. This causes winds to blow in from sea to land during the summer, and these winds bring rainfall. The different heating and cooling rates of land and sea mean that in the winter the land becomes cooler than the sea. Therefore the sea is a low pressure region and winds blow from the land to the sea. As these winds blow from the interiors of continents they are dry winds. This seasonal reversal of wind direction is the outstanding characteristic of monsoons, and accounts for the wet summers and dry winters. Monsoon winds are similar to a six-monthly version of land and sea breezes, which change direction after 12 hours.

Because the monsoon lands cover great areas, there are variations in climatic conditions. For instance, the north-west winter winds which blow across China are dry, but pick up some moisture whilst crossing

The location of the world's chief monsoon regions.

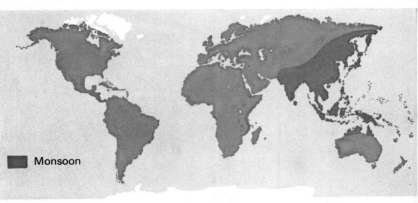

Monsoon

100

the Sea of Japan and bring rain to the western parts of Japan. Near the equator the influence of the doldrum belt and the trades is added to the monsoonal influence, and this accounts for the Indonesian climate and also for the uniqueness of the Indian monsoon.

The most decisive reversal of wind direction occurs in Asia, where the largest continent is adjacent to the largest ocean. Winds blow out in winter and in during the summer much more consistently than in the other continents. In South America, for instance, the continental low pressure draws winds in during the summer, but the narrowness of the continent prevents the temperature from falling too much in winter. The continental high develops though it is feeble, and there are occasions in the winter months when winds blow in and bring rain. Although mon-

soonal in character, this is not a true monsoon and it is better to refer to this type of climate as eastern marginal. Eastern marginal rather than true monsoonal climate also occurs in North America, where the Gulf of Mexico helps to allow warmth into the continent during the winter, so preventing the formation of a very intensive high pressure system.

Temperatures in monsoon or eastern marginal regions range from 30°C in the tropical latitudes to as low as 15°C in Siberia or eastern Canada, because of the latitudinal differences. Winter temperatures range from 20°C in southern India or Indonesia to well below zero in the most northerly areas.

Rain falls in summer, though in eastern marginal areas there will also be some in winter too. The amounts vary from over 10 000 mm at Cherrapunji in the Himalayan

Monthly temperature and rainfall figures at Calcutta, India.

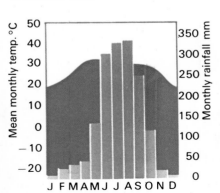

Monthly temperature and rainfall figures at Tientsin, China.

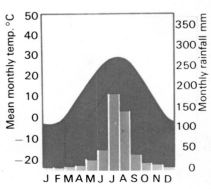

Water being pumped onto fields from a river in India.

forests are not the same as those in equatorial forest regions. With thinner layers of vegetation at the top there is much more under-growth and so, true jungle. Parts of India and elsewhere receive sufficient rainfall for grass but not for trees. Patagonia, the interior of Australia, north-west India and adjacent Pakistan are semi-arid.

India is famous for its monsoon climate, and yet it is different from all others. During the winter the winds blow out and most of India and Pakistan is dry. There are, however, two sources of rain-fall. One is the weak depressions which cross the Middle East from the Mediterranean and bring some light rain to the Punjab; the other is brought by off-shore winds which blow from India into the Bay of Bengal. They are turned to their right by the rotation of the earth and blow back over the coast south of Madras, and across Sri Lanka. The hot season starts in March and con-tinues until May. Temperatures rise to well over 30°C, and low pressure develops, but the equatorial low pressure belt is close to southern India and still attracts the winds. Therefore, there are no on-shore winds and India remains dry. By June the land is so hot, the low pressure so intense, that the winds all turn and blow into India. This happens quite quickly, which is why the monsoon is said to 'burst'.

The rainy season continues until December. Coastal areas and slopes

foothills to less than 250 mm in the Thar desert of India, so it is wrong to assume that monsoonal areas are very wet.

These variations in temperature and rainfall obviously contribute to considerable variations in types of natural vegetation, and also to agricultural possibilities. Much of south-eastern Asia will receive 2000 mm in the summer half of the year, and growth is rapid and pro-lific. The winter months are dry and growth ceases. Therefore, the

Eastern marginal climate. Pampas scene with family of rheas.

facing the winds receive over 2000 mm, but sheltered and inland areas remain very dry. The amount of rainfall is extremely unreliable and famines often occur if there is insufficient rain to water the crops. Where the rainfall is over 2000 mm, dense jungle with palms, bamboo and tree ferns will be found. There are deciduous forests in areas with 1000–2000 mm, and grassland and thorny scrub occur where the rainfall is between 375 and 1000 mm. Less than 375 mm will only support desert vegetation. Where the rainfall exceeds 2000 mm, rice is the main food crop; maize grows well where the rainfall is 1000 mm; and wheat and millet are the staple foodstuffs in the drier areas.

The old peasant way of life still survives in many places, and primitive forms of irrigation such as shallow wells, water wheels or tanks are utilised. Tanks are merely fields surrounded by embankments, and flood water is trapped in these fields. The water level gradually subsides and crops can then be grown. Perennial irrigation can be found in several places now. 'Perennial'

An illustration of dense forest growth in the wet tropical lands.

means that water is available throughout the year, so that crops can be grown in the dry season as well as the rainy months. Water trapped behind dams is led off through canals and taken to the fields wherever required. This type of irrigation costs much money, which is why it is not found everywhere in India.

The monsoons of China give dry north-west winds in winter and wet south-east winds in summer. The winter winds blow out from a very cold area and bring zero temperatures to the northern half of China. Only in the south is crop-growing possible in winter. Summer temperatures reach 25°C in the south, but only 15°C in the north. The rain comes from the east and near the coast 1000 mm are received, but inland the rain diminishes to 250 mm on the edges of the Gobi Desert. The highlands are wetter than the lowlands, because of relief rainfall, and are still forested. Most of the lowlands have been cleared for agriculture. The soils are very rich, especially in the valleys of the three main rivers – the Si, the Yangtse and the Hwang. In southern China rice is the main food, and two or even three crops may be obtained annually. In central China, where rainfall and temperatures are slightly lower, rice and wheat are grown. In northern China there is virtually no rice, and wheat is the main source of food. Some areas are too dry or too cold for wheat, and millet and kaoliang are both important.

The effects of the sea are evident in Japan, which is slightly milder than at comparable latitudes in China. The same winds affect Japan, but some winter rain falls. Southern Japan is warm enough to grow rice with summer temperatures exceeding 20°C, but northern Japan, especially the island of Hokkaido, is too cool and hardier crops are grown. Food supplies in Japan are not solely dependent on climatic conditions – there is much fish available too.

Australia and South America both contain areas with eastern marginal climates. In Australia the eastern coastlands are wet enough to support forest, but the rain shadow effect of the Great Divide prevents much rain from penetrating inland. The interior is grassland at first, deteriorating into desert.

South America has forests in southern Brazil, but grassland in the pampas. This grass is rich and lush near Buenos Aires, but becomes poorer inland and southwards into Patagonia.

Tea plantation on a hillside. Sri Lankan women are picking the leaves.

Maritime

Maritime regions are located on the west sides of continents between 40 and 60° north and south of the equator. The main examples are in western Europe, but there are also maritime regions in British Columbia, Washington and Oregon, Southern Chile, Tasmania and southern New Zealand. The name maritime means influenced by the sea, and therefore in areas such as west U.S.A., where the mountain ranges run north-south, the sea influence cannot penetrate very far inland. In Europe there are few obstacles and so maritime influences extend as far as U.S.S.R.

The influence of the sea makes maritime climates mild and wet. Summer temperatures are never very hot, ranging from 15–20°C. Winter temperatures vary from 0–5°C, which is really very warm for the latitudes. This warmth is the result of westerly weather bringing warm air from the oceans. The outstanding source of warmth is the North Atlantic Drift which affects western Europe.

The rain falls throughout the year, though winter tends to be wetter than summer. The rain is brought by the depressions of the temperate low pressure belt which pass steadily from west to east across these maritime lands. They are more active and numerous in winter, but at all seasons they weaken steadily as they move inland. Rainfall is about 1000 mm on lowland coasts, and 750 mm or less inland. The rainfall is cyclonic in type, but in the mountains it is added to by relief rain fall. Parts of the Scottish Highlands average 4000 mm per annum, as do the Southern Andes in Chile and the Southern Alps in New Zealand.

The mild temperatures and

The location of the world's chief maritime regions.

Maritime

Wellington, New Zealand. View over the port to the interior hills.

ample rainfall enable trees to grow and deciduous forests cover most maritime regions, though much has now been removed for agriculture and settlements. North-west U.S.A. also contains many coniferous trees such as the Douglas fir. The deciduous trees, such as oak, ash and elm, all shed their leaves and have a rest period during the winter months.

The soils which form in these deciduous forest areas are brownish in colour and quite fertile, so high quality farming is widespread. The temperatures limit the crops which can be grown, but wheat, barley, oats, rye, temperate fruits and vegetables are all important. Climatic conditions are excellent for the growth of grass, and so pastoral farming is successful, with cattle and sheep being reared. Maritime regions are very suitable for human beings, and so there are many densely populated areas. This is particularly true of Europe, where large towns and industries abound in the maritime lands.

Monthly temperature and rainfall figures at Seattle, U.S.A.

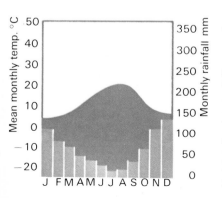

Continental

Continental regions are located in the middle of continents between 40 and 60°N, but do not occur in the southern hemisphere as there is insufficient land in those latitudes. The main regions include the Prairies of Canada and U.S.A., the Steppes of U.S.S.R., and the grasslands of Hungary and Rumania. It is very difficult to draw a dividing line between maritime and continental regions in Europe, as there are no sudden climatic changes. In North America the division is somewhat clearer because of the north-south mountain ranges which act as barriers.

Summer temperatures are about 20°C, slightly warmer than the maritime lands in the same latitude because of the warming influence of the land. Winter temperatures are below zero, because the land mass cools down much more quickly than the sea.

Rainfall is quite low because of distance from the sea, and the annual total is only 375–500 mm. Much of this falls in summer convection storms, and a little falls in winter as snow.

The warm summers, cold winters and low rainfall support grassland vegetation. In more favoured areas of soil and climate a rich cover of grass is found, but elsewhere there is a rather patchy tussocky grass. These lands are the northern hemisphere temperate grasslands.

The original inhabitants in North America were the nomadic Indians. They hunted the buffalo which once roamed the Prairies in millions. There were nomadic hunters and herders, such as the Kirghiz on the Steppes of the U.S.S.R. When settlers moved into these grasslands, from the east in U.S.A. and from the west in U.S.S.R., they found exten-

The location of the world's chief continental regions.

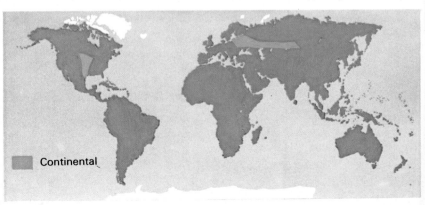

Continental

Combine harvesters at work on the Canadian Prairies.

sive grassland suitable for pastoral farming. Gradually, as the settlers increased, the land was ploughed and cultivated, chiefly for cereals. The soils in the better parts of the Prairies are rich and black because of the dead grass roots. They are called chernozems in U.S.S.R. The drier parts of the grasslands (the west in U.S.A. and the east in U.S.S.R.) have sparser grass and poorer soils. These were also ploughed by land-hungry settlers in U.S.A. in the 1930s. Unfortunately, the crops failed and the soil was exposed and blown away. Serious soil erosion created the gullied Badlands area. The drier steppes were ploughed, but not until the 1950s,

and they have also suffered from erosion. Now, instead of ploughing large areas of land for one crop, farmers are practising mixed farming which is much better for the soil.

Monthly temperature and rainfall figures at Winnipeg, Canada.

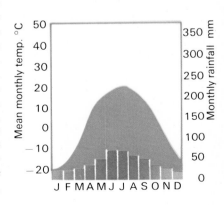

109

Taiga

The taiga, or coniferous forest regions, are located in the northern hemisphere to the north of the continental climates. They only occur in the northern hemisphere because southern hemisphere continents are too narrow, or non-existent in these latitudes. Much of Canada, parts of Norway, Sweden and Finland, and a vast expanse of U.S.S.R. contain coniferous forests.

The climate is really a type of continental, being sunny in summer and very cold in winter. January average temperatures are well below zero – minus 10°C or even lower. This is because of the northerly position and hence low angle of the sun in the sky, and also because of the inland location. Summer temperatures average 15°C, though as the days are very long the sum-

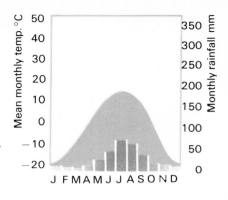

Monthly temperature and rainfall figures at Irkutsk, U.S.S.R.

mer conditions are very pleasant. The heat from the land causes convection currents and occasional summer storms bring most of the rainfall which amounts to about 375 mm per annum. There is a little snow in winter, but the temperatures are too low for heavy falls, and most of the land and the rivers are frozen solid.

The location of the world's chief taiga regions.

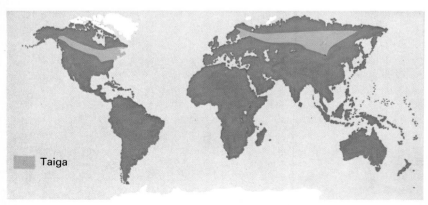

Taiga

Raccoons inhabit many forests in both North and South America.

The taiga produces much sawn timber which is often transported by lorry.

Climatic conditions are very similar to those in the continental grasslands, but the winter temperatures are lower. There is less evaporation here so the rainfall supports coniferous forests, whereas in warmer latitudes it is only adequate for grass. The main trees are spruce and fir, but larch are also numerous and there are often many silver birch, the hardiest of the deciduous trees. Conditions are really too harsh for deciduous trees and coniferous trees are better able to survive because they spread their roots out horizontally instead of vertically. In this way they overcome the problem of frozen ground.

The trees in the taiga become smaller and more widely spaced moving northwards, until they are really only bushes. This is where the tundra begins.

Climatic conditions are not suitable for much agriculture, though hay, potatoes, oats and rye will grow. Most settlements concentrate on dairy farming for fresh milk and grow fodder crops, especially hay, to keep the cattle alive during the winter months. The cattle have to live in cowsheds for about half the year.

The major settlements are associated with forestry, though there are some mining towns too. The trees are mainly cut down in winter and many of the lumberjacks work on their farms during the summer months. Sawmills often use hydro-electric power, and although they produce some sawn timber, the main product is pulp for paper manufacture.

Tundra

The tundra regions are located to the north of the taiga and only occur in the northern hemisphere. There is tundra in Alaska, northern Canada, northern Norway, Sweden and Finland, and the largest area of all is in the U.S.S.R. There are small expanses of mountain tundra in most high mountain ranges.

Climatic conditions are really continental in type. Summers are very sunny, though average temperatures are only 10°–15°C. Long sunny days make conditions quite pleasant. Winter temperatures are well below zero – minus 20°C or even lower – because of the northerly latitude and inland location. The coldest places on earth, excluding the ice caps, are found in the U.S.S.R. tundra. Here, Verkhoyansk averages minus 40°C in

The location of the world's chief tundra regions.

January, though July temperatures are about 16°C. The ground is permanently frozen, and this is known as *permafrost*. In the summer months the sunshine melts the top few centimetres but the water cannot sink underground, because of the frozen rock, and so marshy areas are very common. The boggy tundra landscape swarms with flies and mosquitoes in summer. Large numbers of birds, including many ducks and geese, also spend the summer on the tundra.

The climatic conditions are too severe for trees to grow, though bushes and dwarf willow survive in sheltered hollows and valleys. There are several berry fruits, including cranberries, and many flowering plants appear in the summer. Moss and lichen are the hardy plants which cover much of the surface in the tundra. Reindeer, known as caribou in North America, feed on the moss, although even they migrate southwards in the

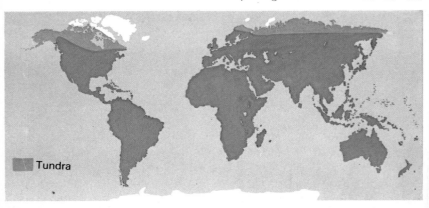

Tundra

A tundra scene in the Arctic showing the barren landscape.

winter. Other animals such as foxes and lemmings are also found in the summer.

Few people live in tundra lands because of the inhospitable climate. Permafrost prevents crops from being grown, though some settlements have glasshouses and grow plants in trays or boxes. Yields then are very high and growth is rapid because of the long sunny days. The few permanent settlements are associated with mining, as at Kiruna in Arctic Sweden where there are large deposits of iron. Schefferville in eastern Canada has vast reserves of iron ore, and Coppermine in north-west Canada has deposits of copper. One of the biggest mineral discoveries has been near Prudhoe Bay on the Arctic coast of Alaska, where enormous oil deposits are being tapped. A pipeline has been built across Alaska to the small ice-free port of Valdez.

The original inhabitants of the tundra have gradually changed their traditional way of life, as a result of increasing interference from outsiders. Some of the Lapps of northern Sweden still herd reindeer, though they do settle in permanent locations such as Jokkmokk for several months of the year.

Monthly temperature and rainfall figures at Verkhoyansk, U.S.S.R.

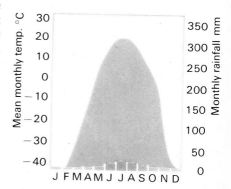

Ice Caps

An eskimo, kayak and iceberg in the Arctic.

The major ice caps are found in Greenland and Antarctica, where they cover the entire landscape and in places reach 3000 metres in thickness. The weight of the ice is such that if all the ice melted the land would rise by more than 300 metres, although at the same time the melting ice would raise sea level by 100 metres or more. This would have very serious consequences for the world's great towns which are on or near the coast.

The ice caps occur in areas with low temperatures even in summer, and therefore the melt rate of snow and ice is slower than the replacement rate. Annual snowfalls are low – only 100 mm per annum – but because the melt rate has been so slow over thousands of years these massive ice caps have been able to accumulate. Winter temperatures are below minus 30°C and there is total darkness. In summer there is continuous daylight and sun temperatures may be above freezing point. The shade temperatures remain just below zero. The cold air which accumulates over the ice caps develops a local high pressure system from which winds blow out. These winds are cold as they travel across the surrounding countryside or ocean. If they are funnelled down valleys and become cold currents of air, often travelling at 20 km/h, they are known as *katabatic winds*.

The location of the world's chief ice cap regions.

Ice cap

ner and there are fewer icebergs. Ice floes are common and they may be derived from the land or consist simply of frozen seawater.

Icebergs are a danger to shipping, as demonstrated by the sinking of the famous Titanic on her maiden voyage in 1912. There is now an International Iceberg Patrol System operated by the U.S.A. Coastguards, which informs all shipping of the position of icebergs in twice-daily reports. There is more of an iceberg below the surface than above, though the exact amount may vary, depending on how much air there is within the ice. Normally ¾ or ⅞ of the iceberg will be beneath the surface.

The only inhabitants of ice caps are to be found at scientific research stations. Notable explorers of Antarctica include Amundsen and Scott. Amundsen reached the South Pole in 1911.

Icebreakers help to keep channels open both in the Arctic and Antarctic.

Monthly temperature and rainfall figures at Mawson, Antarctica.

It is not only air that moves out from the ice caps – the weight and pressure of snow and ice also causes outward movements. If the ice moves as a sheet it may spread on to the sea as a sheet, but if it moves down valleys it will break off in large lumps, or icebergs. Most Greenland ice breaks off in this way and most of the Atlantic icebergs are calved from Greenland's glaciers. In the Antarctic, however, the ice is thin-

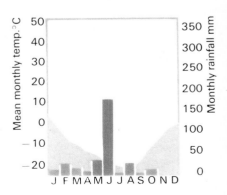

Mountains

Mountain ranges not only develop their own climatic conditions, but may also affect the climate of adjacent areas. For example, the Great Dividing Ranges of eastern Australia help to cause the dry conditions of much of the interior.

The main effect of mountains is on rainfall. Winds blowing on to mountains are forced to rise and as this happens, the air cools. Cooling air can hold less moisture and therefore clouds form and rain will fall. The wettest places in the world, the Himalayan foothills and Hawaiian Islands, are both affected by relief rainfall and annual totals exceed 11 000 mm. In regions such as Britain, where the rainfall in lowlands varies from 625–950 mm, the mountains receive 1500 mm or more. Snowdon, for example, averages more than 4000 mm per annum. Even in deserts, relief rainfall is received; the Tibesti mountains have 400 mm, whereas most of the Sahara receives 200 mm or less.

As the air rises up mountainsides it is cooled and drops rain, but above a certain height, usually 2000–3000 metres, the air becomes so cold that its moisture content diminishes. Therefore the increase of precipitation on mountains has an upper limit above which the rainfall decreases. This height is never reached in Britain, but certainly occurs in the Alps and other high mountains in temperate latitudes. Rainfall also decreases in tropical areas where the rain is convectional in character. Convection currents are caused by heat, so the further up mountains they go, where temperatures decrease, the more they will decrease themselves. So it is that in tropical mountainous areas rainfall, as well as temperature, decrease with height.

The location of some of the world's largest mountain ranges.

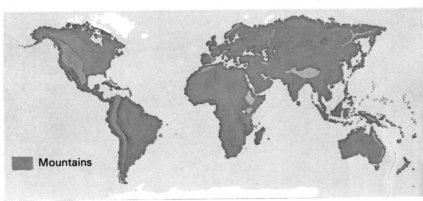

Mountains

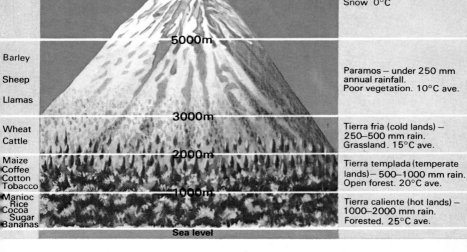

Snow 0°C

5000m

Barley

Sheep

Llamas

3000m

Wheat
Cattle

2000m

Maize
Coffee
Cotton
Tobacco
Manioc
Rice
Cocoa
Sugar
Bananas

1000m

Sea level

Paramos — under 250 mm
annual rainfall.
Poor vegetation. 10°C ave.

Tierra fria (cold lands) —
250–500 mm rain.
Grassland. 15°C ave.

Tierra templada (temperate
lands) — 500–1000 mm rain.
Open forest. 20°C ave.

Tierra caliente (hot lands) —
1000–2000 mm rain.
Forested. 25°C ave.

Climatic and vegetation zones on an
equatorial mountain.

In the Andes of South America
there are distinct climatic and vegetation zones. The lowest 1000

Monthly temperature and rainfall figures
at Quito, Ecuador.

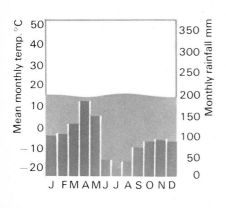

metres is called the *tierra caliente*,
which means hot lands. From
1000–2000 metres is the *tierra templada*, or temperate lands. Between
2000 and 3000 metres is the *tierra
fria*, or cold lands. Above the tierra
fria are the high mountain pastures
which resemble tundra, and they
gradually become colder and more
barren until the snow line is
reached.

Other mountains all show
altitudinal changes of climate and
vegetation. The Alps have forested
zones which tend to be deciduous
lower down, and coniferous higher
up. Above the forest is the mountain
grassland known as alpine pasture,
then the barren tundra rocky zone,
and last of all snow. Even low hills
such as those in Britain contain
woodlands above which only poor
grass, bracken and heather survive.

117

Earth's Resources

Introduction

The resources of the earth include not only minerals and forests, but also soil, water and air. Some of these can be used and re-used, if carefully looked after. Others, such as minerals, will eventually run out. Soil may be lost, but can slowly be re-made; the quantity of water is fixed, though there will be variations in available water dependent on how much is locked up in ice caps.

In the past anyone wishing to use a resource has gone right ahead and used it, if he was able to obtain it. Sometimes this meant very rapid use and even exhaustion of resources, such as minerals or forests or soil. During the twentieth century there has been a rapid increase in consumption rates, and in many cases Man has been extravagant and wasteful.

Mining is a robber industry; once taken away, the mineral cannot be returned. Many minerals will be exhausted early in the twenty-first century at present rates of consumption. It is difficult to be very precise about exhaustion rates, as new deposits may still be discovered and lower-quality ones may become economically worthwhile. For example, only copper ore of 2% purity used to be mined, but now many mines extract copper of less than 1% purity. This means that for every 100 tonnes of rock dug up, less than 1 tonne will be copper.

Forestry and fishing have also been robber industries in the past, as trees were cut down without thought for the future, and seas were fished indiscriminately. Nowadays planning has overcome these problems: re-afforestation ensures that new trees are planted to replace those which are being cut down, and limits have been placed on mesh sizes for fishing nets, so that some fish are spared to breed for future generations. Also, fish farms and special breeding areas have been created – as, for example, in Lim Fjord, Denmark, and in some Scottish lochs and inland ponds.

Soil has been protected in many areas by more thoughtful use of the land, especially by the introduction of crop rotation methods. If different crops can be grown, instead of the same crop year after year, the soil does not become exhausted. It is useful to keep the soil covered for as long as possible, so that it will not be blown or washed away.

Exhaustion Dates of Minerals
(assuming current usage rates)

By A.D. 2000:	*Before A.D. 2100:*
Gold	Copper
Lead	Nickel
Silver	Molybdenum
Platinum	*Before A.D. 2200:*
Zinc	Aluminium
	Manganese
	Cobalt

Soils and Erosion

Soil is very slow to form, and what may take 1000 years to accumulate may all be lost in a few minutes in one heavy rainstorm, or one very windy day. It is very important to protect soil from erosion, which may be sheet or gully form. It normally results from the inefficient or thoughtless use of the land by removal of the vegetation and the exposure of the soil.

Ploughing removes the vegetation, and soil can be blown or washed away if plants do not grow quickly to hold it together. If too many animals are carried on any land they may eat all the vegetation and expose the soil to erosion. This is called overgrazing and, with ploughing and the removal of forests, contributes seriously to soil erosion.

In sheet erosion the fine particles of top soil are all blown away to reduce the soil to an infertile condition. This happens in dry areas, and occasionally during dry spells in wetter regions. For example, the Fens of England lose much fine soil during windy weather in spring, before the vegetation has grown to hold the soil together.

Gullying is caused by rapid movements of water. Once started, gullies are enlarged to form a landscape like that of the Badlands in parts of the High Plains of U.S.A.

Badland erosion in the High Plains of U.S.A.

Agricultural Commodities

Rice is the main cereal of tropical lands. It grows in areas of high temperatures (20–25°C) and high rainfall (over 1000 mm), and is often found on rich alluvial soils of river valleys and deltas. The major producing countries are: China 115 million tonnes per annum, India 61 million, Indonesia 22 million, Bangladesh 17 million, Japan 16 million, Thailand 13 million, Burma 8 million.

Most of the producing areas are densely populated – for example, in the Ganges delta of Bangladesh, or the Si delta near Canton in southern China. Therefore, there is little rice to sell, though Thailand and Burma have small exports. Rice is often grown on terraced hillsides, and is usually found in small fields. There is little mechanised rice cultivation and most of the planting and harvesting is done by hand, using the same methods as in the past. Some rice growing areas are able to grow two or three crops each year by using small nursery areas. In the nurseries, seedlings can be grown so that when the first crop is harvested they are ready to be transplanted into the fields.

Maize is the main cereal of sub-tropical lands. It grows best where the summer temperatures are about 20°C and where the rainfall is 750–1000 mm. U.S.A. produces 118 million tonnes per annum, most of which is grown in the corn belt of the

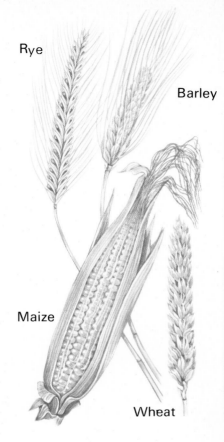

Rye

Barley

Maize

Wheat

The seeds of four of the world's temperate cereals.

Mississippi Basin. Maize is often known as corn, and is the source of corn-on-the-cob. China produces 31 million tonnes, Brazil 16 million, U.S.S.R. 12 million, South Africa 11 million, Argentina 10 million and France 9 million. Much Maize is grown for fodder, especially in

U.S.A. and Argentina. In the U.S.A. it is fed to pigs and cattle, and the Argentine maize is exported to Denmark, Britain and elsewhere for use as cattle feed. Most other countries grow maize as human food, especially in Africa where it is made into mealies, the staple diet of the Bantu.

Wheat is the most important cereal of temperate latitudes, and grows best where the summer temperatures are between 15 and 20°C and the rainfall is 375 to 625 mm. The main producers are U.S.S.R., with 83 million tonnes, U.S.A. 48 million, China 37 million, India 22 million, France 18 million, Canada 14 million, Australia 11 million, and Turkey 11 million. On the Steppes of Russia and the Prairies of North America some wheat is planted in

Women working in Japanese rice paddy fields.

the spring and harvested in late summer. This is known as spring wheat and requires 100 frost-free days between the last killing spring frost and the first autumn frost. In areas with mild winters the wheat can be planted in the autumn and harvested in early or mid-summer. This is known as winter wheat and gives a larger yield per hectare than spring wheat. Much wheat is grown on large farms which are highly mechanised. There is a large export of wheat, in contrast to rice, as much is grown in sparsely populated areas such as the Prairies of North America, the Pampas of Argentina and the Murray lowlands of Australia.

Barley is grown in temperate latitudes in U.S.S.R. 54 million tonnes, China 20 million, France 10 million, and U.K. 9 million. It is used as animal fodder and also for beer. Oats are grown in U.S.S.R. 15 million tonnes, U.S.A. 9 million, and Canada 3 million, and are used as fodder. Barley can survive in drier and colder conditions than are required for wheat, and oats can survive in wetter conditions. Rye is a hardier crop than these other cereals and is grown in U.S.S.R. 15 million tonnes, Poland 8 million and West Germany 2·5 million.

Potatoes are a very important food crop in many countries, and are also used as a feed for animals and a source of industrial alcohol. U.S.S.R. produces 80 million tonnes, Poland 52 million, China 38

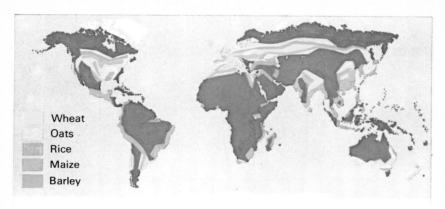

Some major growing areas of the important cereals.

million, U.S.A. 15 million, West Germany 14 million, East Germany 11 million, France 7 million and U.K. 6 million. They grow best in heavy soils in temperate climates. Able to withstand low temperatures and heavy rainfall, they grow well in parts of Scandinavia and Ireland, respectively. They are a staple foodstuff in Ireland, and in many higher settlements in the Andes. There are now potato picking machines, but many producers still use slow hand harvesting methods.

Beet and other root crops grown as fodder are quite similar to potatoes in climatic requirements, but sugar beet is slightly more demanding. Rich soils are essential and sunny summers with average temperatures of 15–20°C help to increase the sugar content, thereby bringing more profit to the farmer. U.S.S.R. grows 76 million tonnes,

France 22 million, U.S.A. 20 million, West Germany 16 million and Poland 12 million. The sugar beet has to be refined very quickly as the sugar content starts to diminish immediately the root has been dug up. The refineries are located in the growing areas such as the Fens of England or the lowland areas of the North German Plain.

Market gardening is an important branch of farming and includes the growth of early potatoes, green vegetables, tomatoes, berries and currants. Climatic conditions have to be suitable for the growth of these crops, and there must be local markets. As many market gardening crops are perishable, they are frequently grown near large towns where they can be sold quickly. Glasshouses are often used for growing tomatoes, flowers and vegetables, especially in the Netherlands and the Lea Valley north of London. Market gardening, which is known as truck farming in U.S.A., is usually important in areas with mild winters where crops can be grown and sent to market earlier than those from the normal producing areas. Cornwall in Britain and Florida in U.S.A. are both important areas.

There are many types of fruit which can be grown in different climatic environments. Soft fruit (berries and currants) and tree fruit (apples, plums, pears) are grown in temperate climates such as Britain. Citrus fruits (oranges, lemons, limes) are grown in Mediterranean and sub-tropical climates such as Italy, Spain, Israel, Australia, California and Florida. Tropical fruits such as bananas and pineapples are grown in the West Indies and elsewhere. Dates are grown in desert regions. Egypt produces 380 000 tonnes per annum, Iran 350 000, Iraq 320 000, Saudi Arabia 260 000, Algeria 180 000, Pakistan 141 000, Sudan 100 000 and Morocco 92 000.

Sugar cane requires a tropical climate for successful growth, as frost is harmful to it. The plant is really a thick grass containing a sweet juice which can be extracted by crushing and squeezing. It

Labourers at work picking oranges in an orchard in Israel.

Cutting sugar cane in Queensland, Australia.

requires 1500 mm of rain per annum and monthly temperatures over 20°C. The main producers are India 137 million tonnes, Brazil 95 million, Cuba 60 million, China 40 million, Mexico 37 million, Pakistan 23 million, U.S.A. 23 million and the Philippines 23 million. Once cut, the cane has to be refined quickly to avoid loss of sugar. It is often grown on large plantations where light railways are used to transport the cane from fields to factory. The factories can use the waste products as fuel, and may also turn out rum and molasses in addition to sugar. The cane is often cut by hand, though machines are used in some places such as southern U.S.A. and Queensland, Australia. Much sugar is exported from Brazil, Cuba and the Philippines, especially to Western Europe and North America.

Another crop exported from the tropics is bananas. The main growers are Brazil 7 million tonnes, India 3 million, Ecuador 2·8 million, Indonesia 1·9 million, Burundi 1·5 million and Honduras 1·3 million. Large-scale production methods are necessary, as for sugar cane, but, in addition to operating large plantations, the banana companies need special refrigeration boats to carry the bananas to markets. South and Central America send bananas to Europe, and they have to be picked green enough to be ready for eating a few days after they arrive. They are stored in special warehouses and can be brought out and sent to shops as required.

The main non-alcoholic drinks are tea, coffee and cocoa. Cocoa is a tropical forest crop requiring rainfall every month (about 2000 mm per annum), and temperatures of 25°C every month. The cocoa tree produces pods on the trunk and main branches. These contain the beans which are the source of cocoa to drink, and also chocolate. Ghana produces 380 000 tonnes per annum, Nigeria 230 000, Ivory Coast 220 000 and Brazil 196 000. Much is exported to Western Europe.

Coffee requires less rainfall and lower temperatures than cocoa – 1000–1500 mm and 20–25°C, respectively. It grows in savanna and tierra templada regions. Naturally, the coffee plant would grow into a tree, but it is normally pruned down to a bush. Each bush contains many beans which have to be picked and dried. The main producers are Brazil 1 620 000 tonnes, Colombia 520 000, Ivory Coast 300 000,

Grape vines are trained to grow up stakes and along wires.

Angola 220 000, Mexico 210 000 and Uganda 200 000. Much is exported to Western Europe and North America.

Tea needs temperatures of 20°C and a heavy rainfall (over 2000 mm), but well drained soil. Therefore hillsides are frequently used for tea plantations. The bushes yield several pickings, or flushes, of leaves. India produces 490 000 tonnes per annum, China 320 000, Sri Lanka 201 000 and Japan 97 000.

Hops are used for making beer and vines yield the grapes for wine. The main wine producers are France, with 82 million hectolitres, Italy with 76 million, and Spain with 39 million.

Crushing grapes in a wooden tub to squeeze out the juice.

Cattle are widespread as they can survive in a variety of climatic environments. India has 179 million cattle, U.S.A. 127 million, U.S.S.R. 106 million, Brazil 88 million, China 63 million, Argentina 58 million and Australia 30 million. India's cattle are of poorer quality and do not yield much milk or meat, but in U.S.A. beef and milk are important products. The more fertile cattle areas where feed is abundant tend to be used for fattening beef before slaughtering – as in the Midlands of England, or in the U.S.A. Corn Belt.

Dairy cattle are found in areas with rich pastures such as southwest England, Denmark or New Zealand, or near large towns where there is a good local market to buy the milk. Surpluses of milk can be turned into butter or cheese. The leading butter producers in the world are U.S.S.R., France, West Germany, India, U.S.A., Poland, East Germany and New Zealand. The leading cheese producers are U.S.A., India, U.S.S.R., France, West Germany, Italy and Netherlands. The leading beef and veal producers are U.S.A., U.S.S.R., Argentina, Brazil, France, China and Australia.

Sheep are not very numerous in the tropics but can survive in cold mountainous areas and dry semi-arid regions. They thrive in rich farming areas such as the English Midlands or Canterbury Plains in New Zealand. The poorer areas are used for rearing wool sheep and the richer areas for mutton. Most sheep are now dual-purpose, yielding good quality wool for 2 to 3 years and then being slaughtered for meat. Lambs are often fattened and slaughtered when they are about 9 months old. Australia has 145 million sheep, U.S.S.R. 142 million, China 72 million, New Zealand 55 million, Argentina 41 million, India

Cattle are reared in most of the world's grassy environments.

Pigs have large families and are an important source of human food.

40 million, Iran 38 million, Turkey 36 million, South Africa 31 million and U.K. 28 million.

U.S.S.R. produces 1 million tonnes of mutton and lamb, New Zealand 493 000, Australia 465 000, China 327 000, U.K. 251 000, and U.S.A. 213 000.

While cattle and sheep are rather fussy about where they live, pigs can survive anywhere. They are mostly found in densely populated areas, near good markets and where waste human food is available. China has 239 million pigs, U.S.S.R. 70 million, U.S.A. 61 million, Brazil 34 million, Poland 21 million, West Germany 20 million and Mexico 13 million. Pork is produced by all these countries in large quantities. Denmark specialises in bacon, and U.S.A. and Brazil produce most of the world's lard.

All animal farming comes under the heading of pastoral farming, and mainly concerns cattle and sheep. There are also other important animals in special localities – for example, the yak in Tibet, the llama in the Andes, the reindeer in the Arctic, and goats in Mediterranean countries and elsewhere.

Sheep shearing is mostly done by shearers who move round from farm to farm.

Minerals

Minerals have a fairly uneven distribution throughout the world, and they can be considered as a kind of geological lottery. Some countries have been very fortunate.

Coal, oil and natural gas are normally found in sedimentary rocks, but most other minerals form in igneous or metamorphic rocks. These rocks are associated with heat and pressure which cause heated liquids and gases to pass through the rocks. These liquids and gases change existing minerals and form new minerals, some of which will be metals or precious stones. Because most of the minerals are formed in similar ways, it is quite common to find several types close together in the same area.

Iron is the most important mineral after the power sources, and the world's main producers are U.S.S.R. 135 million tonnes, Australia 59 million, U.S.A. 47 million, Brazil 40 million, China 40 million, and Canada 30 million. The ore may be only 25% pure, but is normally 50–70% pure and has to be purified before it can be turned into steel. Many iron mines are quite close to the surface and the ore can be obtained by quarrying or opencast methods. This is easier and cheaper than having to sink shafts, but it makes a mess of the countryside. Some of the large iron mining countries use all their iron, but others have exports. The big Australian mines in the deserts of Western Australia send much ore to Japan; Canada sends ore to U.S.A. and Britain from the new mines near Schefferville on the Labrador–Quebec border. Britain also imports iron ore from Sweden, Spain and Sierra Leone.

Copper is produced mainly by U.S.A. with 1 446 000 tonnes; U.S.S.R. 1 200 000; Chile 902 000; Canada 826 000; Zambia 698 000; Zaire 544 000; Australia 256 000 and Peru 213 000. It is mainly used for copper wire and in electrical industries, but the world's copper supplies are running out, and substitute materials will have to be found early in the twenty-first century. It is possible to re-use scrap, though it is often expensive. Copper is often mined in fairly difficult areas – for example, Broken Hill and Cloncurry in Australia, both of which are connected to the coastline by long railways. The copper belt of Zambia and adjacent parts of Zaire also has to be connected to the coast by long railways. Copper is sometimes obtained from underground mines, but is often quarried in deep pits on the surface. There are mines in the deserts of Northern Chile, and also 3000 metres up the Andes at Chuquicamata.

Tin is a fairly heavy mineral which can sometimes be obtained by panning or dredging from old stream beds. Heavy minerals such as tin, platinum or gold will be left behind as deposits or residue, whilst

An open-cast iron ore working in Western Australia.

other lighter minerals may be washed away. In Malaysia much tin is obtained from old river deposits, whereas in Bolivia most tin is obtained by the normal mining methods. Malaysia produces 68 000 tonnes per annum, Bolivia 29 000, Indonesia 25 000, China 23 000, and Thailand 20 000. Much tin is exported from these countries to North America and Western Europe. It is mainly used for plating sheets of steel, but a little is still used as an alloy for making bronze and pewter.

Lead is often found with zinc. The main producers are U.S.A. with 602 000 tonnes, U.S.S.R. 590 000, Australia 377 000, Canada 296 000, Mexico 218 000, and Peru 193 000. Lead is quite soft but is resistant to corrosion, and is used as a roofing material and in making pipes and paint; a little also goes into petrol. It is now known that if too much lead from the atmosphere accumulates in the bodies of fish, animals or human beings, they will suffer from lead poisoning.

Zinc is mainly produced in Canada 1 122 000 tonnes, U.S.S.R. 950 000, Australia 454 000, U.S.A. 449 000, Peru 387 000 and Mexico 263 000. It is used for galvanising iron and steel products and as an

Mule emerging from a tunnel at Pilgrim's Rest gold mine in Transvaal where some primitive methods are still used.

alloy in brass. Large sources of lead and zinc are found at Broken Hill in Australia, Broken Hill in Zambia and Kootenay in British Colombia.

Bauxite is the mineral which is used for making aluminium – the most commonly used metal, apart from steel. The main sources of bauxite are Australia, 20 million tonnes, Jamaica 15 million, Guinea 7 million, Surinam 6 million, and U.S.S.R. 6 million. Much is exported, especially to Japan, North America and Western Europe.

Aluminium works are often situated near hydro-electric power stations, as much electricity is required. Arvida in eastern Canada, and Fort William in Scotland are two locations.

Special steels are made by the addition of small quantities of minerals to ordinary steel. For instance, the addition of manganese makes a very hard and tough steel. Nickel steel is strong and non-magnetic and chrome steel is stainless. Chrome is chiefly mined in U.S.S.R. and South Africa, nickel in Canada, New Caledonia and U.S.S.R., and manganese in U.S.S.R., South Africa and Brazil.

Phosphates, potash, salt and sulphur are important minerals with a variety of uses. Phosphates are used as fertilisers and are mainly mined in U.S.A. with 38 million tonnes, U.S.S.R. 21 million, and Morocco 17 million. Potash, another source of fertilisers, comes from U.S.S.R. with 5 million tonnes, Canada 4 million, West Germany 2·9 million and East Germany 2·5 million. Salt is an important source of chemicals but is also used in foodstuffs. The U.S.A. mines 39 million tonnes per annum, China 18 million, U.S.S.R. 12 million, U.K. 9 million and West Germany 8 million. Sulphur is also important to chemical industries and may be obtained from volcanic sources, from pyrites or as a by-product of natural gas refining. U.S.A. produces 7 million tonnes, Poland 3 million, U.S.S.R. 2·3 million, and France 1·8 million.

Gold, silver and platinum are known as precious metals. Gold is used in jewellery, and South Africa produces 855 000 kg, U.S.S.R. 400 000 kg and Canada 59 000 kg. Silver mainly comes from U.S.S.R. which produces 1500 tonnes per annum, Canada 1300, Peru 1260, Mexico 1168 and U.S.A. 1052. The main use is in ornamental work and jewellery.

A huge pit created by machines digging out large quantities of copper ore.

Power

A fuel such as coal is used to provide power or energy. The main sources of energy are the fuels, man and animals, wind, nuclear and solar energy, tidal and geothermal energy, and water. Most important are the three minerals – coal, oil and natural gas – and water. Coal provides nearly half of the world's energy, oil about one-third, natural gas about 15% and hydro-electric power less than 10%. Much of the energy now comes in the form of electricity.

Wood and water were early sources of power, but with the industrial revolution and the development of steam power, coal became the major source. Coal consists of the decayed remains of vegetation, and when consolidated it forms a sedimentary rock. Conditions have to be just right to enable the vegetation to turn into coal. The plants have to be tree ferns, which live in warm climates, and when they die and accumulate on the ground, they must be covered by sediment fairly quickly, before the bacteria can destroy them and make them rot away.

Different conditions and types of vegetation cause the formation of different types of coal. Coal, like oil and natural gas, is called a *hydrocarbon*, and consists of varying amounts of carbon, oxygen, hydrogen and nitrogen. Anthracite is a hard coal which is more than 90% carbon. It burns with little flame but gives great heat, and leaves little ash behind. Bituminous coal is 70–90% carbon and is quite smoky, leaving ash behind. Lignite, or brown coal, is 45–65% carbon. It is brown in colour, gives off less heat than bituminous, and leaves more ash. Peat is not coal, but contains about 30% carbon and is inferior to lignite as a source of heat. The main producers of coal are U.S.S.R. 684 million tonnes per annum, U.S.A. 542 million, China 428 million, Poland 162 million, U.K. 110 million and West Germany 100 million. The main lignite producers are East Germany 247 million tonnes, U.S.S.R. 172 million, West Germany 126 million and Czechoslovakia 82 million. Lignite is normally turned into electricity near the mines, or used in local industries. Coal is used in blast furnaces and many other industries and for domestic heating. It is also an important raw material for chemicals, being a source of ammonia, plastics, nylon and many other commodities. There is now only a limited trade in coal. Poland, in particular, exports a few million tonnes. There is much movement of coal within countries, from a mining area to a large industrial region. For example, the coal of the Kuznetsk area in Siberia is sent over 1500 kilometres to the steel producers in the Ural region.

There was a large trade in coal during the early years of the twentieth century, when Britain was the main exporter. 1913 was the peak year with over 200 million tonnes being exported, but there was a steady decrease thereafter. The decline in exports resulted from other countries exploiting their own resources of coal, developing

Vertical section to show coal seams and the different methods and equipment used for extracting coal.

seams vertical shafts are sunk. If the coal seam outcrops on a valley slope, the mining can work into the hillside horizontally, and this is called *adit mining*. If the coal is near the surface it can be dug or quarried without going underground. This is called *open-cast mining*.

Oil and natural gas are not solid and so they are brought to the surface in different ways. Holes are drilled down into the ground to reach

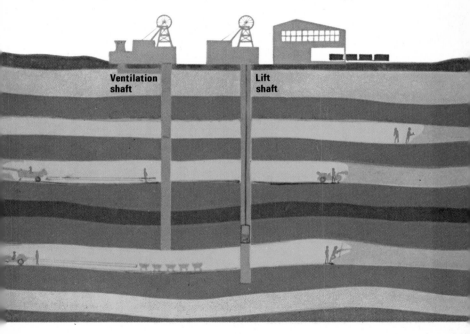

Ventilation shaft

Lift shaft

hydro-electric power, or utilising petroleum or natural gas deposits.

Coal, like other solid minerals, can be mined in one of three ways. In order to reach underground

the liquid or gas trapped in sedimentary rocks below the surface. Petroleum and natural gas are both hydrocarbons and are formed from plant and animal remains

An old source of energy (for grinding corn) which may become important again.

oil are U.S.A. 498 million tonnes per annum, U.S.S.R. 456 million, Saudi Arabia 409 million, Iran 301 million, Venezuela 154 million and Kuwait 114 million. The natural gas producers are U.S.A. 617 000 million cubic metres, U.S.S.R. 261 000, Canada 86 000, Netherlands 83 000, and U.K. 32 000.

The world demand for oil and gas has increased steadily during the last thirty years and most of the easily accessible reserves are being tapped or have been exhausted. Hence the search has gone on to more hostile environments. On the large new oilfields near the north coast of Alaska men have had to overcome problems of severe cold, and in the North Sea they have had to cope with fierce winds and waves.

Many large inlets have become important ports because of oil. For example, Rotterdam – already important – has become the biggest port in the world with the growth of Europoort, which can handle some of the largest tankers. Milford Haven in Wales and Loch Long in Scotland are important because the water depth is nearly 20 metres, which enables 300 000-tonne tankers to sail into sheltered water for unloading. These two locations are not in industrial regions, so pipelines and smaller tankers are required to transfer refined products to markets.

which have accumulated in geological traps. Gas and oil are often found together.

Once obtained, the crude mineral needs refining and in many cases refineries are great distances away from the mining areas. This is because the industrial countries which buy the oil from the producing countries find it cheaper and more convenient to refine their own oil. This has given rise to the great tankers which sail from the Middle East to Japan and Western Europe, and on many other routes too. There are also lengthy pipeline links transporting oil, gas and their refined products across countries such as Britain, France, U.S.S.R. and U.S.A. The main producers of

Hydro-electric power station and cross section of dam and power house showing water flow, generator and turbine.

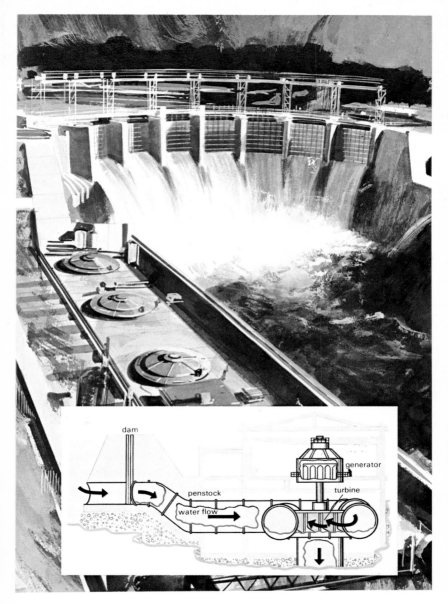

dam

generator

penstock

water flow

turbine

In addition to the hydrocarbons there are other sources of power: hydro-electricity and nuclear power, wind, tides and the sun. Hydro-electric schemes require a large flow of water which must be regular and be moving swiftly down a steep gradient. This fast flow is called the head of water; it may either be a very fast natural stream or it can be created by having a power station a

Nuclear power station at Dounreay in Scotland. Nuclear energy is becoming more important in the advanced countries.

the Alps at the end of the nineteenth century. Most modern hydro-electric power schemes are multi-purpose, which means that they provide electricity and also irrigation water, or improve navigation or provide flood control. The Aswan dam on the Nile and Grand Coulee in north-west U.S.A. are examples of large multi-purpose schemes. Large quantities of hydro-electricity are produced in U.S.A. and U.S.S.R., but both these countries have other sources of energy. Switzerland, Sweden and northern Scot-

few hundred metres below a lake from which water can be piped down steeply. Water power has been in use for many centuries, to turn wheels and drive mills, but hydro-electricity as such was only developed in North America and

land are areas where hydro-electricity is vital because there are no alternative sources of energy. It is the wet, mountainous areas with heavy rainfall and steep slopes which depend almost entirely on hydro-electric power.

There is not much hope of increasing the output of hydro-electric power dramatically, and as coal, oil and natural gas will run out, possibly in the twenty-first century, alternative sources of power are required. Wind can be harnessed on a small scale, and windmills have been used for centuries. Tidal power might be useful though uneconomic at present. There is a tidal power station on the river Rance in northern France. Nuclear power uses uranium and is already quite important in some countries such as U.K., U.S.A., France and Japan. But the uranium will eventually run out, and there are no safe ways of disposing of large quantities of radio-active waste. Solar energy may provide the ultimate solution, although at present no large-scale schemes are economical. However some houses and a few hotels have experimented fairly successfully in obtaining heating from the sun's rays.

Thousands of small mirrors focus heat into one point to create solar energy.

Industries

There are many different types of industry, all of which need some power or energy to work the machines. In the past, when domestic industry was most important, human beings provided the power – to drive a spinning or weaving machine, for example. Windmills and water wheels also provided energy, and wood was burnt as a fuel. With the Industrial Revolution near the end of the eighteenth century there came a great change, as machines became much more widespread and steam power became available. The coal necessary for steam power was common in Britain, helping to account for Britain's lead in industry at that time. All the industries which developed in the nineteenth century – notably steel, textiles and engineering – were located on or near deposits of coal. The coalfields became the centres of industry and grew into densely populated areas which were normally dirty because of the coal dust and waste products from industries. The Black Country of England, between Birmingham and Wolverhampton, earned its name because of this. Many of these old industrial areas still show signs of those former days, and many have now decayed into poor areas in need of re-development. Some old mining areas have been sown with grass and turned into parks, some have been developed as industrial museums, but some still remain an eyesore.

In the twentieth century many industries have developed away from coalfields. For example, iron deposits have attracted some industries, e.g. Corby, or Scunthorpe in England. Ports have become big industrial centres because of the availability of imported raw materials. Hydro-electric power stations are also locations for industries such as aluminium works which require much power. Some light industries have developed near large towns because of the availability of a labour supply and also a good market for selling the product, and some industries just develop because the people concerned happen to live in that particular place. For example, a man called Morris (later Lord

An aluminium works near Reykjavik, Iceland.

A furnace for melting rock (ore) to turn it into steel.

Nuffield) lived in Oxford and so the motor car industry developed there.

One of the biggest of all industries, and the source of many other industries, is steel making. The raw materials required are iron ore, coal to provide heat, and limestone to line the furnaces. Before the Industrial Revolution, charcoal was used as fuel and therefore forests were necessary. Iron-stone was the other requirement, and so iron industries developed in the Weald of south-eastern England and elsewhere. With the development of steam power, the steel industries really grew on the coalfields, as the coal was the bulkiest raw material.

The iron has to be melted down to remove all the impurities, making pig iron, which is the half-way stage between iron ore and steel. Further purification turns the pig iron into steel. Bessemer, Gilchrist, Thomas and others made inventions which improved the efficiency of steel production, and new steel works now have electric furnaces. Modern mills are very large and contain all the processes in one factory; iron, coal and limestone are put in at one end and finished products, such as sheets of steel, girders or motor cars, come out at the other end. This is known as *integration*. These integrated steel works, such as at Port Talbot in Wales, are very large and need enormous quantities of raw materials. There is nowhere in the world which has all the materials in sufficient quantities, and so the import of one or more materials is necessary. The cheapest form of transport for bulky commodities is by sea, which is why most of these new integrated works are situated on the coast. The major steel producers in the world are: U.S.S.R. 135 million tonnes per annum, U.S.A. 131 million, Japan 117 million, West Germany 53 million, China 28 million, France 27 million, Italy 23 million and U.K. 22 million.

Steel manufacture provides the materials for many other industries such as shipbuilding, engineering and cars. Shipbuilding is a large-scale industry which must be near

An automated car assembly plant in northern Italy.

A paper mill, one of the great consumers of the world's forests.

supplies of steel, but must also be on deep and sheltered water. Some of the old coalfield areas near the coast, such as Glasgow in Scotland and Newcastle in north-east England, became successful shipbuilding areas, and for much of the twentieth century Britain produced most ships. After World War II the British shipping industry declined because the shipyards had not been modernised. New, efficient shipbuilding companies grew up in many ports such as Hamburg in West Germany and Göteborg in Sweden, but the most successful

also found near ports or near densely populated areas which represent good markets for selling the finished products. Machinery and tools of all kinds are made. The Merseyside area of England is a particularly good engineering region with numerous advantages such as local coal and steel, a good port at Liverpool for import and export, and good local markets in the cotton industry which requires much machinery.

Motor cars are a branch of engineering, though the location is not always easily explained. The Birmingham car factories are well sited for receiving products from the engineering works of the Black Country. Oxford developed because of one man, and Ford at Dagenham grew because of the river Thames for ease of transport, and the ample flat land for erecting the large buildings. In U.S.A. the main car centre is Detroit, which grew because it

country has been Japan. Osaka and Yokohama both obtain steel from nearby steelworks and produce many ships, including oil tankers of 200 000 and even 300 000 tonnes. Japan produces 15 million tonnes of shipping per annum, of which 59% is tankers. Sweden is the second producer in the world with $2 \cdot 5$ million (55% tankers), and West Germany third with $1 \cdot 9$ (41% tankers). Spain, producing $1 \cdot 5$ million tonnes (65%), France $1 \cdot 1$ (57%), Norway 1 million (54%) and U.K. 1 million (35%) are other shipbuilding nations.

Engineering industries are often located near steelworks which can provide the raw materials. They are

The I.C.I. works in Billingham, England, producing chemicals.

Like all large cities, San Francisco contains many industries.

was the home of Henry Ford. It was also well placed to receive steel from local factories. Another important car area in U.S.A. has been created near Los Angeles for political reasons, in an attempt to move some car works away from the Detroit and Great Lakes area.

A very important industry for the developed countries of Western Europe and North America is paper-making, because of the requirements of the newspaper industry. Softwood from coniferous trees is the main raw material, and much has to be exported from Scandinavia, U.S.S.R. and Canada. Canada produces 8·1 million tonnes of newsprint per annum, U.S.A. 3 million, Japan 2·1 million, Finland 1·3 million, U.S.S.R. 1·2 million and Sweden 1 million.

Softwood is also used for rayon, a product of one branch of the chemical industry. Chemicals are very varied, but vital to most other forms of industry. Products range from plastics to medicine and clothing. The location of chemical industries is determined by the availability of raw materials, labour and markets. There are chemical works on coalfields in Lancashire; near deposits of salt on Merseyside and Teesside; near supplies of sulphur at Houston, Texas; where there are supplies of potash or phosphate, as near Stassfurt in East Germany or at ports such as Liverpool; and near markets such as textile industries or any large town.

Textile industries are often very old, for example in Flanders and northern France. Woollen and linen goods, using sheep's wool and flax, respectively, were the oldest materials, but cotton became important with the creation of plantations in southern U.S.A. in the seventeenth century. The twentieth century has seen the growth of synthetic fibre industries using chemicals, oil, coal or wood as raw materials. Woollen industries tend to be found in areas which are very good for rearing sheep such as the Cotswolds in England. They have also developed where coal and steam powered the machines used to produce large quantities, as in Yorkshire. Other West European countries, as well as U.S.A., U.S.S.R. and Japan, are the major producers of woollen goods. The same countries, and China and India, produce cotton goods too. Highly mechanised factories are now necessary for textile manufacture, though some old small industries survive in the west of Scotland and elsewhere, producing high quality goods such as Harris tweed.

Most industrial development is associated with large-scale factories now, and vast amounts of building materials are required. Chalk and limestone quarries, and sand and gravel pits, are a vital aspect of all forms of industry.

Bulldozer at work in a sand quarry providing essential building materials.

Water

Water is a vital resource, possibly only exceeded in importance by air. It is essential to humans and is also used in agriculture, industry, the home, as power, for transport, recreation, disposal of sewage and fire fighting, to name only a few. The amount available on earth is fixed, though at times more may be stored in the ice caps as well as in the sea, lakes, rivers and rocks. There is no real world shortage but there are often serious regional or temporary difficulties. In order to control the use of water, authorities often demand payment, especially in areas which regularly have water shortages.

The uneven distribution of water means that in many places surplus water is running to waste. This might apply generally to equatorial areas such as the Amazon Basin, or seasonally as in India and Bangladesh. These two countries have regions which are sometimes flooded disastrously in the wet season, when water runs to waste, but in winter there may be serious water shortages.

A surplus and a shortage may occur in different parts of a country at the same time. In California, canals transfer water from the wetter north of the state to the drier south. The U.S.A. is investigating a scheme to transfer water from the Arctic regions of Canada, where demand for water is small, to the drier States of western U.S.A. Even in Britain, which is really a wet country, there are big differences between the west, where rainfall may reach 5000 mm, and the south-east with only 600 mm. There are several schemes for piping water from the Welsh highlands to urban areas in England, such as Birming-

Water is used for fighting fires. This Canadair CL 215 is a water bomber in action over a forest fire.

Sprinkler irrigation in Israel. The pipes are moved from one field to another.

ham and Liverpool. Some urban areas find it more difficult to obtain their water, and both Los Angeles and Kuwait have investigated the possibility of towing enormous icebergs from Antarctica to provide their fresh water.

The distribution of water is determined by rainfall which is extremely varied, and the rate at which water runs off on the surface or sinks into the ground. Much water is lost by evaporation, especially in hot dry areas where the need for water is often very great.

Evaporation may amount to 500 mm, even in England, and could reach 2000 mm in South Africa and elsewhere.

The demand for water is determined by population, standard of living, and also industrial development. Large industries use as much water as a village or small town, and in advanced countries the people use much more water than in primitive communities.

The main sources of water are springs, wells, rivers, lakes, artesian wells and reservoirs. A little is now obtained from the distillation of seawater, as, for example, in the Canary Islands and Kuwait.

Forests

Forests formerly covered a much greater area than at present. They have been cleared to create agricultural land and settlements, but have also been used for building, fuel, pulp, paper and rayon. Trees also provide other products such as gum, rubber, cork and flavourings.

Over one quarter of the land surface is still forested. The major areas are the tropical forests of the Amazon, Zaire and south-east Asia; the temperate forests which are deciduous or mixed, and are located in monsoonal, Mediterranean and maritime regions; and the coniferous forests of the taiga region. Many mountains are forested, although the surrounding lowlands may be grassland.

Tropical forests are largely unexploited because the trees are very mixed, and trees of the same species are widely dispersed. Also, the tropical countries have little labour, communications or money to spend on the forestry industry. Some special hardwoods, such as teak or mahogany, are obtained – often with the help of elephant labour as in south-east Asia. Large areas of forest are now being cut down to create farming land or to make roadways, and this wholesale destruction of forest might affect the oxygen content of the air, and possibly even the world climate.

The temperate forests contain both hard and softwood. The hardwood trees yield oak, walnut and others for furniture-making, and also provide nuts. The softwoods are used for constructional purposes and for pulp and paper. Large expanses of forest are found in southern Chile, southern New Zealand, Washington and Oregon, British Columbia and parts of western Europe.

The location of the world's major forest regions.

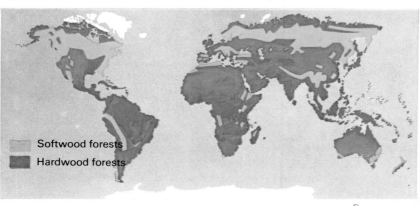

Softwood forests
Hardwood forests

Transplanting seedlings in a nursery, using a portable screen as windbreak.

The taiga occurs in Canada, Norway, Sweden, Finland and U.S.S.R. Vast numbers of coniferous trees are cut down for constructional purposes, furniture, pitprops – but mainly for pulp and paper.

Other useful products from trees include rubber, medicines such as quinine from cinchona, bamboo, tar, maple syrup, chicle for chewing gum, tannin and fruits, nuts and berries. There is a large trade in forest products other than pulp, paper and sawn timber.

During the twentieth century vast areas of forest have been cut down, but now in most countries there are schemes of re-afforestation. This means planting new trees to replace those which are being cut down. Re-afforestation often takes place in the areas from which trees are being cut, but also sometimes in new areas. The new areas are often regions of poor soil such as sandy heathland, or highland regions. The Forestry Commission in the U.K. has utilised thousands of hectares of poor land in this way, in order to maintain and even to increase the supplies of wood.

Fire is a serious hazard, and in large forests there are normally wide avenues which act as safety lines to prevent fires spreading over even greater distances. Canada and other countries have look-out towers from which a watch can be maintained throughout the hottest weather to alert fire-fighting teams as quickly as possible.

The major producers of coniferous wood are the U.S.S.R., with 319 million cubic metres, U.S.A. 272 million, Canada 112 million, China 82 million, Sweden 51 million, and Finland 31 million. The major producers of deciduous or broad-leaved wood are Brazil 137 million cubic metres, Indonesia 134 million, India 112 million, China 100 million, U.S.A. 83 million, U.S.S.R. 64 million and Nigeria 59 million.

People of the World

Introduction

The population of the world rose slowly until the twentieth century, and in recent years the growth rate has increased sharply. The main reason for the recent rapid increase has been the improved medical treatment and the elimination of some diseases. The main increases are now in Asia, South America and Africa, whereas in North America and Australia the increases are slower, and in Europe very slow indeed.

Of the earth's land masses, approximately one-fifth is covered by ice, another fifth is affected by

Country	Total Population (millions)	Population Density per sq. km.
Bangladesh	74	521
Netherlands	13	398
England and Wales	49	326
Belgium	9	316
West Germany	62	249
U.K.	56	230
India	586	178
China	824	86
Scotland	5	66
U.S.A.	211	23
Sweden	8	18
U.S.S.R.	252	11
Australia	13	1·7

Population and population densities.

permafrost, another fifth is arid, and another fifth is mountainous. This leaves one-fifth for people, showing that most of the world's people live in the favoured parts of the world. Average population densities of the continents show considerable variations, but even in individual countries there are great variations from one area to another.

China, for example, which is noted for its high population density, has an average of only 86 people per square kilometre. The mountains and deserts of China contain lands with 1 person to each square kilometre, whereas some of the rich agricultural lands of the Si delta near Canton have 800 people per square kilometre. Egypt's average density is 36 per square kilometre; most of the country is Sahara desert with less than 1 person per square kilometre, but the Nile valley has 500 people living on most square kilometres.

An exponential curve showing world population growth.

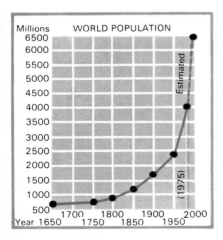

148

Densely Populated Areas

Densely populated areas are those which contain several hundred people per square kilometre – Macao (16 000 per square kilometre), Monaco (12 000), Gibraltar (4500), Hong Kong (4047), and Singapore (3826) are small, densely populated city-states which can support large numbers of people because of industries and trade. Other larger areas support high densities of population because of industrial development which has grown up on coalfields. Many old coal mining areas such as the Ruhr in West Germany, Northern France near Lille, South Wales and north-east England near Newcastle, have become very important for steel, engineering and chemical industries. The availability of jobs attracted many people to these areas, and so groups of towns have grown up very close to each other.

Some areas such as the Si and Yangtse valleys in China, the Ganges delta in Bangladesh, or large parts of Java have become densely populated because of agriculture. Intensive farming in small fields enables a high yield to be obtained from each hectare and this supports densities of 500 per square kilometre or more. Rice is the main crop and its growth is aided in the river valleys by floods which deposit silt annually. In Java there are fertile river soils (alluvium), fertile soils on weathered lava, and numerous terraces which allow crops to be grown on steep slopes. Intensive farming in Java helps to support a population of 80 million on 130 000 square kilometres – just over 600 per square kilometre. Java is part of Indonesia which has an average population density of only 70.

Hong Kong. View over Causeway Bay to city and hills.

Sparsely Populated Areas

Sparsely populated areas are those which contain less than 5 people or even less than 1 per square kilometre. Australia, with 1·7 per sq. km, Botswana 1·1, Canada 2·5, Chad 3·1, Greenland 0·02 and Libya 1·1 are a few examples. These sparsely populated areas are usually very dry, very cold, or very mountainous. There are also many other regions, but not entire countries, which are sparsely populated.

The world's equatorial forests support only a few people, because of the high humidity, disease and dense forest. Lack of good farmland and of minerals has never encouraged large-scale settlement. The Amazon Basin contains between 2 and 3 million people in 5 million square kilometres.

Desert areas are invariably empty lands. The Sahara contains a few nomadic Arabs and some oases, and the Australian desert contains some aborigines. Even in areas with minerals, which give rise to towns such as Kimberley or Kalgoorlie, the average population density is still very low. Therefore not even mineral wealth can create high population densities in the desert lands.

Other empty areas are the cold lands of the tundra in U.S.S.R. and Canada. These areas contain many minerals but as there can be no permanent agriculture the growth of large towns has been prevented. Iceland is more favoured than most regions in high latitudes because of the moderating influence that the sea has on the land, making sheep farming possible. The sea also provides man with an important occupation and a source of food. Even here the density is only 2·1 per square kilometre.

Mountainous areas also support low densities because of the lack of soil, the difficulties of communications and the harsh climate.

The tropical forests only contain small and isolated settlements.

Races

The word 'race' should be used with reference to physical characteristics such as skin colour, hair type, facial appearance and physique.

There are three main racial groups and two smaller groups. The main groups are the Caucasoid, Mongoloid and Negroid. The Caucasoid are white and contain Europeans and many other varied groups, including the Arabs. Mongoloid are yellow and take in the Chinese and all the American Indians, including Eskimos. The Negroid are black and originated in Africa, but have now spread to the Americas and Europe. The smaller groups are the Australoid who are the natives of Australia, and the Capoid who are yellowish-brown and include the Bushmen of South Africa. The pygmies and related groups of Negritos probably form a sixth group, and there are many people in south-east Asia who cannot be easily classified.

There are more Caucasoids than any other group, although the Mongoloids are now nearly as numerous. The Negroid are numerically a poor third. There are very few Capoids and Australoids. All groups are mixing now, especially in South America, and sub-groups and hybrids are gradually evolving. As inter-marriage (miscegenation) increases, the distinctive features of each racial group will disappear.

Some different facial characteristics.

'Red Indian' Negro Hindu

Mongoloid Negroid Caucasoid

Australoid

Japanese Aborigine S. Albanian

Religions

Religions are very varied and range from primitive tribal beliefs to the principal religions of more advanced countries. These are Christianity, Islam, Hinduism, Buddhism, Judaism, Shinto, Confucianism and Taoism.

Christianity started at the time of Christ and has approximately 100 million believers. Of these, over half are Roman Catholic, over one quarter are Protestant and the remainder belong to the Orthodox Church. The Roman Catholics are found in Europe and also in Latin America. The Orthodox Church broke away from Rome in the eleventh century and is well represented in eastern Europe and parts of southern U.S.S.R. The Protestant Church developed from the sixteenth century onwards and is found mostly in Europe, as well as in North America and Australasia.

Islam developed because of Mahomet who lived from 570–632 A.D. After he died the faith of Islam, or Mohammedanism, spread rapidly across North Africa and Western Asia. There are now over 420 million believers.

The Jews were driven out of Palestine in the first century A.D. and spread over the whole world. There are only about 13 million supporters of Judaism; not more than 2 million live in Israel, which was created in 1948 in the area of their former homeland.

Hinduism has over 400 million believers, mostly in India. The caste system divides the people into different groups and has a major effect on ways of life. The Hindu religion does not allow its believers to slaughter cattle, so the millions of cows in India do not help to solve the food shortages.

The minaret (or tower) on a moslem mosque is often highly decorated.

Language

Language is very important, as it enables people to communicate.

There are over 3000 different languages within less than 20 language groups. For example, Indo-European includes all the European languages, Chinese, Ural-Altaic, Niger-Bantu, Hamitic-Semitic, American-Indian and Malay-Polynesian. Language differences have often caused political problems – as in Canada or Belgium at the present time.

Europe contains over 30 languages including the Teutonic, Greek, Latin and Celtic groups. The Latin or Romance languages are Italian, Spanish, Portuguese, French and Rumanian. The Teutonic or Germanic group includes English, German, Dutch, Flemish and Scandinavian.

Spanish, French, Portuguese and English were spread through the world by colonising powers and, with Arabic and Russian, have become the major international languages. The chief commercial languages are English, French, Spanish, German and Russian. Russian is really restricted to U.S.S.R. and east European countries, and German is largely restricted to Europe, though it is an international language for scientists. Spanish and Portuguese are found throughout Latin America, and French is found in north and central Africa, Canada and southeast Asia. English is the most widespread, occurring in Britain, North America and the former colonial territories.

It is estimated that less than 400 million people speak English, yet more than 700 million people speak Chinese. Next in numerical importance are French, Spanish, Italian, Hindi, Russian, Arabic, Urdu, Japanese, Indonesian, Portuguese, German and Bengali. Each of these languages is spoken by over 50 million people.

Languages often coincide with political and racial boundaries.

The distribution of some of the world's major languages.

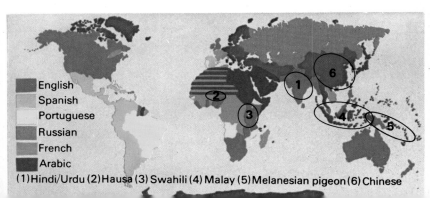

English
Spanish
Portuguese
Russian
French
Arabic

(1) Hindi/Urdu (2) Hausa (3) Swahili (4) Malay (5) Melanesian pigeon (6) Chinese

Tribes

There has been a great variety of tribal groups living in different parts of the world. Many have now disappeared as civilization and outside influences have spoiled the old ways of life. Many tribes have been killed off by warfare or disease. Minor European complaints such as influenza or measles have often proved fatal to tribes which have had no resistance to these illnesses.

There are still small numbers of primitive peoples living in their traditional way. Although regarded as primitive, many of these groups have to be very efficient to survive in difficult environments. For example, the pygmies survive in the hot wet tropical forests, the Bedouin in the Sahara, Aborigines in the Australian desert, and the Eskimos in Arctic Canada, Greenland and Alaska.

The Eskimos are hunters and gatherers and live mostly near the coast so that they are able to catch fish and seals. They live in stone and earth dwellings which are made airtight and draught-proof. During hunting expeditions they live in tents which have been made from skins; some Eskimos build igloos, but most prefer their tents.

All their requirements – food, clothing, fuel for lamps, and tools – are produced from animals which they have caught. The clothing and boots are fully weather-proof and able to resist sub-zero temperatures.

As a contrast, the inhabitants of the equatorial forest wear little clothing, and any dwellings they have serve as a shelter from rain rather than as a protection from cold. The natives of the forests may be hunters and gatherers, or cultivators, as both types of people can survive in these forests. Savanna regions also contain different types of people – notably, the herders such as the Masai and the settled cultivators such as the Kikuyu and Baganda.

Eskimo women and children in parkas.

Migration

Emigrants are people who leave countries and *immigrants* are the people who enter countries. Emigrants may choose to depart for one of a number of reasons – it could be because of difficult climatic or social conditions, disasters, lack of work, religious or political persecution. On the other hand, the attraction of something better in a new country may be the reason for migrating.

One of the earliest countries to send out migrants was Norway. The Vikings sailed away looking for more land and riches to plunder. They reached Iceland, Greenland and North America before Columbus. They also settled in Britain.

From the sixteenth century onwards Spanish and Portuguese settlers began to develop South and Central America, and in the seventeenth century the British and French moved into North America. The development of plantations in U.S.A. and Latin America caused the growth of the slave trade, which was a compulsory form of migration from Africa across the Atlantic for 40 million negroes.

In the nineteenth century, the migration from one continent to another was greater than ever before. Europe provided the emigrants and they went to North America, South America, Australia and New Zealand. High emigration rates from Europe continued until about 1960.

There have recently been movements within Europe – for example, Italians moving to Switzerland and Germany, and Turks going to Germany and Belgium. Many Poles work in Belgium, Algerians in France, and Spaniards in England.

There are also examples of internal migration – for example, southern Italians to northern Italy, and Scots and northern English to the London area.

Things to do

● How many different types of face can you see in your town? Look for racial characteristics.
● How many different churches are there in your town? Can you find out any interesting points about their history?

Early migrants had to be brave, determined and adaptable.

Transport

The History of Transport

Methods of transport have changed steadily during the last two thousand years, and the changes have accelerated during the last one hundred years.

Primitive man depended on the dug out or birch bark canoe and crude rafts to travel over water, while on land it was usual to walk. Donkeys, horses and, in certain areas, camels, yaks or llamas, were then used for carrying possessions or humans. The first wheels are thought to have been developed by Bronze Age people about 1000 or 2000 B.C. The ancient Britons certainly used carts and chariots, but the wheel did not become widespread throughout the world until the Middle Ages.

The Romans were known for their skill in building roads, but in the Middle Ages the roads were poor. Thomas Telford (1757–1834) improved many roads by using layers of stone as foundations, and

digging drainage ditches at the sides. John Macadam made further improvements at the end of the eighteenth century, and the surfaced roads became much more widespread.

Water travel is very ancient, and the oceans used to be crossed by small open boats. Phoenicians traded in the Mediterranean over 2000 years ago, and the Vikings crossed the North Atlantic. Sailing boats were predominant until steam power was developed in the early nineteenth century.

Canals came into use at the end of the eighteenth century and railways followed in the early nineteenth. High speed trains and the monorail are the latest developments in rail transport. With the luxury liner the Q.E.2, Concorde aircraft, hovercraft and other modern forms of transport, much progress has been made since the days of the dug out canoe.

Transport systems have been improved because of scientific and technological changes, but also because of the increased trade between countries. People and commodities move around the world much more freely nowadays.

Indians of North America built their canoes from birch bark.

River

River transport has progressed from primitive birch bark canoes to large pleasure steamers and trading vessels which sail the Rhine, Mississippi or Amazon. Much local traffic can still be found on most large rivers. On the Amazon for example there are many small canoes which serve individual families. There are also boats belonging to traders who travel from one settlement to another. The outboard engine has made great differences to the speed and ease of river travel. There are large river steamers near Belem at the mouth of the Amazon, and occasional ocean-going vessels sail from Liverpool to Manaus. However, there is really very little large-scale traffic on the Amazon because it flows through a sparsely populated and economically poor area. Therefore no one has much produce to sell and no one has money available to import goods.

The Rhine provides a marked contrast with the Amazon as it is only a small river, and it passes through a densely populated and economically advanced region. Rotterdam at the mouth of the Rhine is the largest port in the world. It imports many cargoes which are transferred to river barges and then taken upstream to Cologne, Strasbourg or even Basle in Switzerland, which is the head of navigation. The Rhine suffers from variations in flow such as high water in spring when melt water from Alpine snow comes rushing down; but work is being done to overcome problems in this region.

Riverboat in New Orleans. Many boats ply up and down the Mississippi.

Canals and Lakes

Many rivers are easily navigable, but they are often made much more useful by the presence of canals and lakes. For example, canals link the Rhine to the Rhone, and the Danube to the Ems. Many rivers are said to be canalized when they are deepened and straightened to improve navigability; this is true of the Rhine and the Moselle. Europe contains many canals and North America has a small number, but there are few in the other continents – except where they are used for irrigation. Europe has most canals because it is a densely populated continent and there is a need for bulky commodities such as coal and iron to be transported. The canals of the Netherlands are also useful for drainage.

A distinctive type of canal is that which provides oceanic links, such as the Kiel, Panama or Suez. These were built to shorten the journeys of ships and facilitate world trade. Suez links the Mediterranean with the Indian Ocean and is a sea level cut, but the Panama Canal linking the Pacific and the Atlantic, has locks to enable ships to pass through a low range of hills.

Canals which handle more traffic than both the Suez and Panama are the Soo Canals which link Lake Superior to Lake Huron. These are two of the five Great Lakes which are important for shipping, allowing Chicago to receive ocean-going vessels. No other lakes have as much traffic, but Victoria, Titicaca, Malawi, Nasser and Windermere handle some trading and also pleasure craft.

Panama Canal. A large container ship passing through a lock on the journey to the Pacific.

Sea

Ocean travel began with people drifting on rafts and using large rowing boats, often with slave oarsmen. The success of rafts has been demonstrated by the famous Kon-Tiki expedition. Oars were gradually replaced by sail power, paddle steamers (as on the Mississippi) and then steam power from coal. Oil has now taken over from coal, and there are a few vessels using nuclear power – for example, a Soviet ice-breaker and U.S.A. submarines.

The chief ocean-going vessels in the first half of the twentieth century were tramp steamers which plodded slowly from port to port carrying a variety of cargoes, and returning to their home port perhaps once in every two years or so. Much of this trade has now disappeared with the development of containers. Small cargoes are now packed into containers in factories and can then be loaded directly onto ships – much time is saved by this method. Ships which needed more than a week in port to unload and re-load can now be serviced in one or two days.

The tramps and container vessels represent only a small percentage of the tonnage of vessels afloat because of the oil tankers and a few bulk iron ore carriers. As a result of the growth in oil trade since 1950, tankers now account for more than 50% of all ocean vessels. Another recent change has been the decline of ocean liners, as passengers now travel mostly by air. A few liners such as the Q.E.2 still exist for luxury cruises.

The steamship Great Britain was built by Isambard Kingdom Brunel more than one hundred years ago.

Roads

The old Roman roads were well known for their straightness, and their modern-day equivalents are the motorways or autobahnen.

Roads in Europe and much of North America tend to be surfaced, and the roads are of varying widths and qualities. Britain has a very dense road network with 343 686 kilometres of road in an area of 244 000 square kilometres. This includes the motorways, 'A' roads, 'B' roads and minor roads. There is normally no charge for travel on British roads, although there is a small number of private roads on which payment is necessary, and there are a few toll bridges such as the Severn bridge and the Saltash–Plymouth bridge. Tolls are much more common in Europe and North America, where a fee for travel on the superbly maintained highways is normal. The Highway of the Sun, which runs the length of Italy, is one of Europe's newest major routes, and is a toll road. Europe's oldest major routes are the German autobahnen which were constructed under the Hitler regime in the 1930s to allow the rapid movement of troops and equipment.

Good roads do make travel faster, though most parts of the world now have speed limits. Both in Britain and the U.S.A., the usual limits are 60 or 70 m.p.h., but most other countries express their limits in km/h. Another variation between the countries is that in most cases driving is on the right hand side of the road. Britain, Australia and a few other members of the Commonwealth still drive on the left. It has been suggested that these countries should fall in line with the rest, but the change from left to right would be very difficult and expensive. Sweden made the change in 1967.

The countries with the highest density of roads are the highly populated and industrialised ones. Belgium has 12 830 kilometres of main road in an area of 31 000 sq. km, but

The Romans often used flat stones to surface their roads.

A large articulated lorry in Guadalajara, Mexico.

Uruguay has only 7820 km of highway in an area of 178 000 sq. km.

Roads in and near urban areas tend to be better than those in rural areas, and even in Asia and South America they are generally surfaced. There are a few outstanding long distance roads which have been constructed for political links or to help open up new areas. The Pan American highway is continuous from Fairbanks in Alaska through Canada, U.S.A. and Central America into Colombia. There is a slight gap in Colombia because of difficult terrain and forest, but the highway then continues to Puerto Montt in Southern Chile, with branches leading off to several capital cities. There is an impressive highway leading inland from Magadan on the east coast of Siberia, and there are roads leading from Brasilia across empty forest lands. The most dramatic Brazilian road is the trans-Amazonia highway which travels from the Atlantic coast of Brazil westwards into Peru.

Such long distance roads are cheaper to build than railways, though less efficient for the fast transportation of bulky cargoes. It is also cheaper to build roads than railways in mountainous areas, as they can cope with gradients more easily. The greatest advantage of road travel, though, is flexibility as cargoes can be carried from door-to-door. Obvious disadvantages include traffic jams and the restricted size of cargoes.

Railways

The development of railways began early in the nineteenth century. A steam engine was used in the coal mining region of South Wales in 1804. George Stephenson opened the Stockton–Darlington line in 1825, and the Liverpool–Manchester line in 1830. There was a boom in railway construction during the 1840s and the part played by the railways in the growth of industry during the nineteenth century was invaluable.

Some parts of the world notably Western Europe, have dense networks of railways. Many areas such as the Pampas or eastern U.S.A. have several railways. Large areas have isolated railways, and most parts of the world have no railways.

When railways were built in the nineteenth century they were usually built by companies who were competing with rival concerns. So it is that neighbouring railways are often of different gauges. In Australia, some of the states used different gauges because of interstate rivalry. The trans-continental line from Perth to Sydney has now been converted to standard gauge but formerly, different trains had to be used for different parts of the journey. The trans-continental line from Buenos Aires to Santiago in Chile looks a superb line on a map, but on the ground it actually involves the use of three different gauges.

Most European railways use the standard gauge, which is 4 ft 8½ in (143·5 cm). Spain and Portugal have a 5 ft 6 in (167·6 cm) gauge, and much of U.S.S.R. has a 5 ft (152·4 cm) gauge. Some countries such as Brazil have railway lines with several different gauges. Most railway lines were built in the 100 years from 1840 to 1940, and there have been few built since World War II. The recent constructions have mainly been by mining companies for the removal of a mineral from a mining area to a port. Most of these have been narrow gauge (usually 1 metre) because they are cheaper to construct than the broader gauges. Vehicles on these lines are less stable and cannot take

Stephenson's Rocket reached 45 km/h when winning a competition in 1829.

The French 'Mistral' train en route from Paris to Lyons.

corners so successfully, but this does not matter for the transport of minerals.

Railways are particularly useful for transporting bulky commodities, and they are also suitable for carrying large numbers of passengers in densely populated areas such as London and south-eastern England. They are rather inflexible, though, as the trains have to stay on the lines. In this respect, road transport has some advantages.

Most railways have been losing money recently, mainly because too many lines were built originally, at a time when road transport, now the main rival, was non-existent. Railway systems have been modernised in an attempt to improve efficiency. Steam engines have largely disappeared, and have been replaced by diesel or electric. Special lines such as London–Manchester, Tokyo–Osaka, or Paris–Marseilles have fast efficient services and can run at a profit.

Britain has 47 121 km of railway in an area of 244 000 sq. km, that is 1 kilometre of line in every 5 sq. km. U.S.A. has 348 000 km in an area of 9 363 000 sq. km, which is 1 kilometre for every 27 sq. km.

The Tokaido Line express in Japan covers nearly 700 kms in 250 minutes.

Aircraft

The history of flying is restricted to the twentieth century and the main development of aircraft has come since World War II. The fastest fighter 'planes during that war were much slower than the slowest present-day jets on regular passenger services.

All aircraft used to be driven by propellers but are now mostly driven by jet engines. Much larger aircraft have been developed over the years, with jumbo jets now carrying over 300 passengers. This seems incredible when one considers that aircraft formerly carried only 20 or 30 passengers. The size of aircraft has created the need for bigger airports and longer runways, which take up many hectares of land. This is why major airports are normally located several kilometres away from city centres. A short flight e.g.

Concorde can fly from London to New York in three hours.

London to Paris, can take the same time as the journey from London Air Terminal to Heathrow airport. Another problem which has grown with the size of aircraft is that of noise, and people living under one of the main flight paths near a major airport suffer seriously from the roar of jet engines. The noise of Concorde, the first supersonic passenger aircraft, is so great that in 1977 it was, for a time, refused permission to land at New York airport.

Aircraft are particularly useful for trade and transporting precious cargoes, such as human beings. With their help explorers, scientists and doctors can now gain access to isolated places.

The U.S.A. uses aircraft to a great extent because it is a large country, and fast travel is essential. It is a wealthy country, too, and passengers can afford to pay the fares. In 1974, U.S. airlines carried 207 million passengers and flew 162 000 million miles.

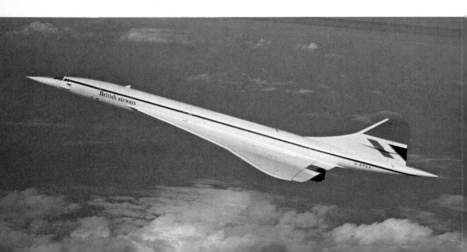

New Communications

Transport and, therefore, communication has progressed steadily since the days of the dug out canoe, and the horse drawn cart. There are many new forms of communication on land, sea and in the air.

In the air there are now helicopters and vertical take-off 'planes, as well as fighter 'planes which can be shot off the ends of aircraft carriers, as though from a catapult. Through the air it is possible to transmit radio messages, and television pictures can be sent round the world via satellites which permanently circle the earth. Telephone and teleprinter can send messages at great speed over long distances.

Hoverlloyd hovercraft on the move.

On land there are new and faster cars, and large freight-carrying lorries or juggernauts. Special express trains often exceed 150 km/h – for example, 'The Bullet' from Tokyo to Osaka covers 500 kilometres in 4 hours.

There are now several monorail services, as in Dusseldorf and at Disneyland in California.

There are various forms of speed boat, and sea and lakes can be crossed by hovercraft and hydrofoil.

Things to do

● Think about local roads, railways and the nearest airport. Is any noise, air pollution or disturbance caused by them? Is there a local traffic problem? If so, how would you solve the problem?

Countries of the World

Facts and Figures

Asia occupies nearly one-third of the world's land and contains more than half the people. It is clearly bordered by ocean in the north, east and south. The western boundary in U.S.S.R. is generally considered to be the Ural mountains. The Caucasus mountains separate European Russia from Asia, and the Straits of Bosphorus are also part of the boundary. The Sinai Peninsula is a transitional area between Asia and Africa.

Asia is a very hot continent in summer but much of it is very cold in winter. It extends from the heights of Everest to below sea level in the Dead Sea, and contains tropical forests and jungles and tundra and ice caps. Asia is a continent of extremes with some very ancient civilisations in both China and Mesopotamia, highly industrialised areas as in Japan, and some extreme poverty in India and elsewhere.

Africa is the second largest continent and extends a similar distance both north and south of the equator. It is a warm continent, as no land is more than 36° north or south.

There are forests on the equator and vast expanses of tropical grassland all around the tropical forest area. The Sahara and Kalahari deserts occupy large areas; the Sahara is much larger than the Kalahari because Africa is wider in the north and there, close to Asia it is drier. Africa was virtually unknown to the outside world until the nineteenth century, and has often been called the 'Dark Continent'. Many countries are still quite poor, though there is much wealth in the Republic of South Africa.

North America is the third largest continent and is surrounded by oceans. The southern tip contains the Central American Republics which link North to South America. The seven Central American Republics have an area of 521 000 sq. km, and the West Indian Islands occupy 168 000 sq. km. North America contains large expanses of forest, grassland and desert. Much of the continent is sparsely populated and although inhabited for a long time by the native Indians, has been settled by white people during the last 400 years. Canada and U.S.A. are both rich countries, but Mexico and Central America contain areas of poverty.

South America is broadest in the tropics and therefore is a fairly warm and wet continent. It does, however, contain the Atacama which is the driest area in the world. The countries of South America are now independent, with the exception of French Guiana, though they were all formerly colonies. Spain colonised most of the continent, though Portugal settled Brazil. There has been much intermarriage between Indians, negroes imported as slaves to work the plantations, and the Europeans. As a result, the people of the South American countries are very mixed and there are few racial problems.

Antarctica is a large land mass almost completely covered by ice, and surrounded by the great Southern Ocean. There are no real settlements in this continent, but merely a few scientific research stations. The climate is so inhospitable that normal life would be quite impossible.

Europe consists of many fairly small countries, but is well populated and well developed. The Mediterranean and Baltic Seas enable oceanic influences to extend far inland and thus it is a climatically mild continent. It is really a large peninsula protruding from Asia, and is broken up by many mountain ranges such as the Alps, Carpathians and Harz Mountains.

Australasia consists of Australia, New Zealand and many islands. Islands to the north represent a transitional area with Asia. New Zealand has strong maritime influences, as nowhere is far from the coast, but Australia is a very dry country. It is in the Horse Latitude regions and the Great Dividing Ranges in the east prevent any wet weather from extending far inland. Thus Australia is sparsely populated in the interior and likely to remain so. Australian settlement was mainly from Britain and began in the nineteenth century.

Here is a useful list of areas and populations of the continents.

Continent	Area (sq. km)	Population (millions)
Asia	43 882 000	2210
Africa	30 284 000	350
North America	24 255 000	305
South America	17 819 000	205
Antarctica	13 338 000	—
Europe	10 497 000	750
Australasia	7 684 000	21

The largest countries of the world are as follows:

Country	Area (sq. km)	Population (millions)
U.S.S.R.	22 402 000	252
China	9 561 000	824
U.S.A.	9 363 000	211
Canada	9 221 000	22
Brazil	8 512 000	104
Australia	7 687 000	13
India	3 288 000	586
Argentina	2 777 000	25
Sudan	2 506 000	17
Algeria	2 382 000	16
Zaire	2 345 000	24
Greenland	2 176 000	049
Saudi Arabia	2 150 000	8

Australia and Greenland are very large islands. There are many other large islands in the world:

Island	Area (sq. km)
New Guinea has an area of	898 000
Borneo	795 000
Baffin	598 000
Malagasy (Madagascar)	590 000
Sumatra	422 000
Great Britain	227 000
Honshu (Japan)	225 000
Sulawesi (Indonesia)	189 000
Prince Albert (Canada)	155 000
South Island (N.Z.)	150 000
Java	124 000

North America

Introduction

U.S.A. contained many different groups of Indians before the arrival of the European. Some lived in the forests of the east, others were on the Prairies, and others lived in semi-arid areas of the west.

European settlement began on the east coast of America in the sixteenth century, but was most rapid from 1850 onwards. The east coast settlements which formed the original 13 states were of British origin. These 13 states are represented by the 13 stripes on the U.S.A. flag. There was a little French settlement in the south and names such as New Orleans remind us of this. Spaniards moved into the south

west via Mexico, as evident from place names like Los Angeles and San Francisco.

Differences between the north and south in U.S.A. led to a Civil War over slavery in the 1860s. Since then the Union has grown steadily and now contains 50 states, each of which is represented by a star on the national flag.

Indian groups of many kinds were present in Canada, too, and the European settlement also came in from the east. The French arrived first and are still numerous in Quebec, but English settlers predominate elsewhere.

Canada consists of 11 provinces ranging from Prince Edward Island which covers 5700 sq. km to North West Territory and Yukon which occupies 3 778 000 sq. km. Transcontinental railways help to link these provinces.

Major towns of North and Central America, and the West Indies.

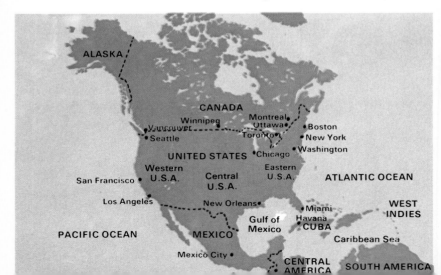

Canada

The Provinces of Canada are as follows:

Province	Area (sq. km)	Population
Alberta	644 000	1 759 000
British Columbia	931 000	2 452 000
Manitoba	549 000	1 016 000
New Brunswick	72 000	673 000
Newfoundland	370 000	548 000
N.W. Territory and Yukon	3 778 000	58 000
Nova Scotia	53 000	821 000
Ontario	891 000	8 200 000
Prince Edward Island	5 700	119 000
Quebec	1 357 000	6 176 000
Saskatchewan	570 000	915 000

The three Atlantic Provinces are quite small and sparsely populated, but are important for some fruit farming, timber products and coal. The Province of Newfoundland includes Labrador which has few people but does contain large deposits of iron ore.

Ontario and Quebec are both well populated in the south, near the U.S.A., but are virtually empty in the north. They use the Great Lakes and St Lawrence for imports and exports, except in winter when this seaway freezes up. Many industries and some mixed farming are found near the Great Lakes.

The three Prairie Provinces contain grassland in the south but are forested in the north. The Prairies are well farmed for cereals but also contain large oil, gas, coal and potash deposits.

British Columbia is west of the Rockies and, although very mountainous, it is a wealthy State with some good farming, vast forests and many mineral deposits. The ports never freeze up in winter.

Mountainous and lake side scenery in the Rockies.

Western U.S.A.

Western U.S.A. contains the following states:

State	Area (sq. km)	Population
Arizona	295 000	1 772 000
California	411 000	19 953 000
Colorado	269 000	2 207 000
Idaho	216 000	713 000
Montana	365 000	694 000
Nevada	286 000	488 000
New Mexico	315 000	1 016 000
Oregon	251 000	2 091 000
Utah	219 000	1 059 000
Washington	176 000	3 409 000
Wyoming	253 000	332 000

Western U.S.A. contains the Rocky Mountains and many other ranges, several areas of high plateaux, and basins surrounded by mountains. The western edge of the plateaux are the Sierra Nevada and Cascade Mountains. Most of the west is arid and covered by scrub vegetation with forests on the highlands. The land is sparsely populated except where irrigation is possible, for example, near Phoenix and Salt Lake City, or where mineral deposits are being exploited. Important mining towns include Butte in Montana and Spokane in Washington. There is much dramatic scenery in these western states, especially the Grand Canyon on the river Colorado, and the Yellowstone National Park in Wyoming.

West of the Sierra Nevada and Cascades there are fertile lowlands and the climate is wetter. Farming and forestry are important. The giant sequoia trees grow in California. Washington and Oregon produce wheat, dairy products and fruits such as apples, pears and some apricots. Hydro-electric

Beach scene in San Diego, California.

power stations are numerous, but Grand Coulee in Washington is one of the largest, and this provides water for irrigation too.

California also grows many fruits and in the south of the State grapes, peaches and oranges are important. There are several rich farming areas in southern California which rely heavily on irrigation. There are oil deposits too, and important industries such as car and aircraft manufacture and film production (Hollywood). The sunny climate which helped the film industries also encourages sunbathing and surfing.

Los Angeles is the main town of California and has a great problem with smog caused by motor car fumes. San Francisco has an excellent natural harbour which is crossed by the Golden Gate bridge. The San Andreas fault, a source of earthquakes, runs through San Francisco.

Nevada has no large towns, though Las Vegas is world-famous as a gambling and entertainment centre. Near to Las Vegas is Lake Mead which has formed behind the Boulder Dam.

Salt Lake City in Utah is the centre of the Mormon religion and has thriving agriculture based on irrigation. Denver in Colorado is another large town which caters for tourists and is a refining centre for metals. Seattle in Washington is located on Puget Sound and has a fine deep water harbour. Besides handling shipping, it is the head-

Golden Gate Bridge in San Francisco with mist caused by the cool sea water.

quarters of the Boeing aircraft industry.

The west of U.S.A. also includes the isolated 49th and 50th states, Alaska and Hawaii. The Hawaiian Islands, at 20°N, have a fine tropical climate, but Alaska contains much tundra and many snow-covered mountains. Alaska has become a wealthy State since 1970 because of the discovery of vast oil deposits.

Central U.S.A.

Central U.S.A. contains the following states:

Name	Area (sq. km)	Population
Alabama	133 000	3 444 000
Arkansas	137 000	1 923 000
Illinois	146 000	11 113 000
Indiana	93 000	5 193 000
Iowa	145 000	2 825 000
Kansas	213 000	2 249 000
Kentucky	104 000	3 219 000
Louisiana	125 000	3 643 000
Michigan	150 000	8 875 000
Minnesota	217 000	3 805 000
Mississippi	123 000	2 216 000
Missouri	180 000	4 677 000
Nebraska	200 000	1 483 000
North Dakota	183 000	617 000
Ohio	106 000	10 652 000
Oklahoma	181 000	2 559 000
South Dakota	199 000	666 000
Tennessee	109 000	3 924 000
Texas	692 000	11 196 000
Wisconsin	145 000	4 417 000

Negro workers on a tractor in the state of Missouri.

The river Mississippi flows through the middle of this region, and it is joined by its large tributaries the Missouri, Ohio and Tennessee. The area is low-lying, bordered by the Appalachian Mountains in the east and the High Plains and Rockies in the west. There are dams on the Missouri which provide water for irrigation, and in the Tennessee Valley there are dams for hydro-electricity.

The rainfall decreases from east to west and the land was naturally forested east of the Mississippi, but was grassland (prairie) to the west. Temperatures decrease from south to north. Near the Gulf coast it is warm enough to grow sugar cane and tropical fruits, but inland in Texas, Mississippi and Arkansas cotton is the main crop. In Kentucky, Tennessee, Missouri and

Montezuma's castle in Arizona. An outstanding Indian cliff dwelling.

Illinois corn (maize) is the main crop, and is grown to feed pigs and cattle. Kansas and Nebraska specialise in winter wheat, but in North and South Dakota and Minnesota, spring wheat is planted because the winters are too cold for winter wheat. The areas of Wisconsin and Michigan are damp and have clay soil – they are used for growing hay and rearing dairy cattle. Much butter and cheese is produced.

There are rich coal deposits in Iowa–Illinois, and large deposits of oil in Texas and Oklahoma. Sulphur and natural gas are found near the Gulf shores of Texas and Louisiana. Although these areas are not densely populated, industries have developed because of the mineral wealth and the high level of farm production. Flour, beef and breakfast cereals are some of the most important agricultural industries, especially at St Louis and Chicago. Chicago is on the Great Lakes system and also has large steel works using iron ore which arrives by boat. Southern towns such as Memphis, Birmingham and New Orleans have cotton industries. Birmingham has local iron and coal deposits which have led to the creation of steel industries. New Orleans is a port, and is the home of Dixieland jazz. Houston is a port and produces chemicals.

Eastern U.S.A.

Eastern U.S.A. contains the following states:

Name	Area (sq. km)	Population
Connecticut	12 000	3 032 000
Delaware	5 000	548 000
Florida	151 000	6 789 000
Georgia	152 000	4 589 000
Maine	86 000	993 000
Maryland	27 000	3 922 000
Massachusetts	21 000	5 689 000
New Hampshire	24 000	737 000
New Jersey	20 000	7 168 000
New York	128 000	18 190 000
North Carolina	136 000	5 082 000
Pennsylvania	117 000	11 793 000
Rhode Island	3 000	949 000
South Carolina	80 000	2 590 000
Vermont	24 000	444 000
Virginia	105 000	4 648 000
West Virginia	62 000	1 744 000

Eastern U.S.A. includes the Appalachian Mountains and the Atlantic Coastal Plain. The lowland area is narrow in New England in the north, but becomes much wider in Georgia and Florida. The climate also changes appreciably between Florida and Maine – the north is well below freezing point in winter, while Florida has January temperatures of 15–20°C.

The mountains are generally sparsely populated and often contain quite poor farming communities. There are many large towns, especially near the coast, and tall skyscrapers are common.

The earliest settlers were farmers but gradually certain industries developed, especially in New England, where the Pilgrim Fathers landed. The northern states concentrate on growing hay and fodder crops to feed animals, especially dairy cattle. The large urban population provides a good market for milk, and also for fresh vegetables which are grown near most towns. A good supply of early vegetables comes from Florida. Florida also grows oranges and limes, and Georgia and the Carolinas grow cotton, peanuts and tobacco.

Southern agriculture is very different from that in the north, and in the past slaves were always used on the southern estates.

The north is more densely populated and contains more towns such as Boston, New York, Philadelphia and Baltimore. These are all ports and large industrial centres. Washington, a large town, is the capital of U.S.A. It was specially located near the dividing line between the North and South at the time of the Civil War, in an attempt to satisfy both sides.

Amish farmer with horses and plough – a member of a small religious sect who reject modern inventions.

The skyline of New York City with many skyscrapers and the river.

Inland in Pennsylvania there are many towns associated with the rich coal deposits. Pittsburgh is the largest, and is a very important steel manufacturer. Buffalo is also a steel producer, as it obtains coal and iron via the Great Lakes. Buffalo is linked to New York by the Hudson Mohawk gap which contains the New York State barge canal. Along this routeway, one of the most important in the U.S.A., are many important towns such as Schenectady, Syracuse, Rochester and Albany, which is the state capital. Further east in the six New England states are many other industrial towns such as Worcester, Providence and Springfield, which specialise in quality goods, textiles, and electrical and engineering products.

The mountains of New England contain ski resorts, and the coast caters for summer tourists, but the major holiday resorts are in Florida – for example, Miami. Florida also contains Cape Canaveral which is the space rocket launching centre, and the Everglades, a wild marshland rich in animal life.

New York, the largest city of U.S.A., and an important sea port, is a racial melting pot containing negro (Harlem), Puerto Rican, Italian, Irish, Jewish and other communities.

175

Central America

Central America includes the following countries:

Name	Area (sq. km)	Population
Belize	23 000	136 000
Costa Rica	50 700	1 921 000
El Salvador	21 000	3 980 000
Guatemala	109 000	5 540 000
Honduras	112 000	2 933 000
Mexico	1 973 000	58 118 000
Nicaragua	130 000	2 084 000
Panama	76 000	1 631 000

Mexico consists of a plateau bordered by the Sierra Madre mountains, with the two coastal plains. The smaller Central American Republics provide a link between Mexico and Colombia. They are a series of volcanic masses, and the whole area is still very active.

In Mexico the coastal areas contain some towns, notably Vera Cruz, a major port, Tampico, an oil centre, and Acapulco, a famous tourist resort. Most of the towns are located on the plateau where climatic conditions are cooler and favourable to settlement. There are also rich deposits of minerals, notably lead, silver, zinc and copper, as at Chihuahua and San Luis Potosi.

The majority of the inhabitants are still associated with farming, however, generally working on large estates. The chief food crop is maize, but cash crops such as cotton and coffee are grown, especially where irrigation is possible. Much of the plateau is too dry for crops and cattle; goats and some sheep are reared on the poor pasture.

The original Indians of Mexico were similar to those throughout the

The ruins of Palenque – an ancient Mayan city in south-east Mexico, discovered overgrown by jungle.

length of the Americas. Two major civilizations had developed before the arrival of the Spaniards in the sixteenth century – the Aztec, near Mexico City, and the Mayan in Yucatan. Indians have intermarried with Europeans throughout Central America and more than half the people are now mestizos, or crossbreeds.

Guatemala has a mountainous backbone, with northern and southern lowlands. Most people are farmers and live in the higher areas, especially at the altitude of tierra templada (see page 117). Maize, wheat and beans are grown as food crops, and coffee is the main cash crop, accounting for over 50% of the national exports.

El Salvador contains a mountain range but only a southern coastal plain. The mountains include Izalco, a volcano which is almost permanently flaming – one of many active volcanoes in Central America. Most people are farmers and maize and coffee are the main crops grown.

Belize was formerly called British Honduras and is a low-lying forested area with much swamp. Sugar cane, citrus fruits and forest products are the main exports.

Honduras contains mineral wealth and fertile soils, but is still the poorest of the Central American Republics. Most farming is for subsistence, maize being the chief crop. Bananas are the main export, and there are plantations on the Carib-

Cowboy in Guadalajara. The hats vary slightly from region to region.

bean coastal plain, financed by the United Fruit and Standard Fruit Companies of the United States. There is a little coffee grown in the highlands.

Nicaragua, Costa Rica and Panama show many similarities to Honduras and Guatemala. The Panama Canal is the greatest source of income in Central America. The Canal links the Atlantic (via the Caribbean Sea) with the Pacific, and Panama receives income from the Canal Zone.

West Indies

The West Indies consist of the Bahamas, the Greater Antilles, the Lesser Antilles, Trinidad and Tobago, and the Dutch islands off the Venezuelan coast. They stretch over 3000 kilometres.

The largest islands are:

Name	Area (sq. km)	Population
Cuba	115 000	9 090 000
Hispaniola	77 000	9 076 000
Jamaica	11 000	1 998 000
Puerto Rico	8 900	3 031 000
Trinidad and Tobago	5 100	1 062 000

They are all noted for sunshine and warmth, as well as ample, often seasonal, rainfall. Vegetation is largely luxuriant. The islands are often mountainous and volcanic, though there are also small, low coralline islands covered with palm trees. They produce sugar and bananas. The people there have a special love for cricket and the West Indies team is one of the best in the world.

Cuba is as large as all the other islands together, and its exports earn more than half the total value of all the small Central American Republics. There are high mountains in the interior, but much productive land on the lowlands. Sugar is the main crop and major export. Fishing is also important and there are deposits of several important metals, notably manganese.

Hispaniola is the second largest island and contains two countries. Haiti occupies one third of the area but has half the population and is rather overpopulated. The people are negroes, descendants of slaves, and French is the main language. Coffee is the main export, and bauxite is second. The Dominican Republic contains more fertile land than Haiti, with some rich sugar estates.

Jamaica is a densely populated island, and farming land is limited. Many people have emigrated to Britain to seek work. The interior is very mountainous, but there are rich agricultural areas around the edges. Sugar and bananas are important, especially in the north which is wetter because it faces the rain-bearing winds. Subsistence agriculture is widespread. Bauxite accounts for half the exports, sugar one quarter, and bananas nearly 10%.

Freshly picked bunches of bananas will ripen on the way to foreign markets.

Barbados scene showing golden beaches and palm trees.

Puerto Rico has been influenced and aided by the U.S.A., and there are now nearly one million Puerto Rican migrants living in the U.S.A. Agriculture is mainly subsistence and a few industries have been started to ease the pressure of population on the land.

The islands near South America are sometimes called the Continental islands. They are isolated mountain blocks and include Aruba, Bonaire and Curaçao, which are Dutch, and Trinidad and Barbados, which are British. The Dutch islands are dry and are mainly concerned with refining Venezuelan oil. Barbados is densely populated and many food crops are grown. Sugar and the sugar products of molasses and rum account for over 90% of the exports. Trinidad also grows subsistence crops and sugar, though sugar accounts for only 5% of the exports. This is because of the petroleum deposits which represent over 80% of the exports.

The smaller islands between Trinidad and Puerto Rico are the Lesser Antilles, with the Leeward Islands in the north and the Windward Islands in the south. These islands are submarine volcanoes, some of which are still active. Sugar, cotton and fruits are grown on small patches of farmed land. The tourist trade is now of great importance.

There are many coral islands in the West Indies, especially in the Bahamas which contain 700, although only 30 are inhabited.

South America

Introduction

South America contains 13 countries:

Name	Area (sq. km)	Population
Argentina	2 777 000	25 050 000
Bolivia	1 099 000	5 470 000
Brazil	8 512 000	104 243 000
Chile	757 000	10 405 000
Colombia	1 139 000	23 952 000
Ecuador	284 000	6 951 000
French Guiana	91 000	58 000
Guyana	215 000	774 000
Paraguay	407 000	2 572 000
Peru	1 285 000	15 383 000
Surinam	163 000	411 000
Uruguay	178 000	3 028 000
Venezuela	912 000	11 632 000

South America contains the long mountain range of the Andes extending from north-west Colombia to the island of Tierra del Fuego. These mountains include several active volcanic peaks, and where the Andes split into two ranges there are inter-montane plateaux between the high mountains. The Andes are young fold mountains, but the other highlands of Guiana and Brazil are relics of old mountains. The north-east corner of Brazil, Cape Sao Roque, used to fit into the Gulf of Guinea in West Africa; this geographical jigsaw was the first evidence that the continents actually moved. The Guiana and Brazilian highlands are similar to old mountains in West Africa. In-between and surrounding the highland masses are the lowland basins of the Orinoco, Amazon and Panama rivers.

Much of South America is tropical, because the wide part of the continent is in the north. The Andes also affect climate and the Humboldt current flowing off northern Chile and the length of Peru causes the aridity of the Atacama desert.

The tropical lowland areas are sparsely populated and most people live in the elevated tropics or in the more temperate southern parts. The original inhabitants, the Indians, came to South America via Bering Straits and North America, several thousand years ago. They were spread fairly thinly over the continent when the first Europeans

Major cities of South America.

180

Market in Ecuador showing the colourful clothes of the inhabitants.

started to settle in the sixteenth century. There were primitive groups of Indians in the Amazon forests and more advanced tribes such as the Incas living in the Andes. The civilisation of the Incas was very highly developed, but was totally destroyed by the Spanish in the sixteenth and seventeenth centuries. There were Indian groups living by hunting on the Pampas, and others on the coast of Chile who were fishermen.

The earliest European settlers came to seek for gold and silver, or to spread the gospel – or just to win glory by capturing land for Spain or Portugal. As a result of a decision by the Pope in 1494, Brazil was settled by the Portuguese, but otherwise the Spanish had first claim to the land. Intermarriage with Indians was common, as there were few European women amongst the early settlers. The resulting cross-breeds are called 'mestizos' and are now the most numerous group in South America. As agriculture developed, negro slaves were imported, especially into Brazil, and there was more intermarriage. The negro-European cross-breed is called a 'mulatto'. The result of this cross-breeding is a very mixed group of people, but there are few racial problems and no racial discrimination. The Brazilian football team normally shows a range of skin colours from light to very dark.

Brazil

Brazil consists of 21 states and is correctly known as the United States of Brazil. The Amazon occupies nearly one half of the country and the Brazilian Plateau nearly one third. The remainder is the Atlantic Coastal Plain and the southern three states of Panama, Santa Catarina and Rio Grande do Sul. The Amazon Basin is covered by tropical forest and contains few people. There are isolated small settlements near the rivers, and they collect nuts or rubber from the forests. Manaus (280 000 inhabitants) is the main inland town, and Belem (570 000) is a large port near the mouth. They both serve as market centres for the surrounding lands. In order to attempt to open up the Amazon Basin, and to encourage settlement, a road has been built from near Belem, running westwards to the Peruvian border.

The Brazilian Plateau is quite densely populated in the south-east, near Sao Paulo, but is sparsely peopled in the interior. In an attempt to encourage settlers to move inland, a new capital city was created at Brasilia in 1960. It now has over ½ million inhabitants. Sao Paulo (5·2 million) and Rio de Janeiro (4·3 million) are the largest cities in Brazil and are located in the wealthiest part of the country. Rio is the leading port, and was the capital

Looking down on Rio de Janeiro, the former capital of Brazil.

Amazon scene with a manatee or sea cow found in some tropical rivers.

until 1960. It is a large industrial town, though Sao Paulo is even more important. The state of Sao Paulo became world famous in the nineteenth century for its coffee production. Other crops such as cotton, tobacco and sugar cane are also important. This part of Brazil has several hydro-electric power stations, large deposits of iron near Itabira, and many other minerals. It contains many industries, quite good road and rail communications, and is far more developed than most parts of South America.

The east coastal plain contains a few isolated towns such as Salvador (1 million), and Recife (1 million). These are very old settlements first set up by the Portuguese in the sixteenth century. There are rich sugar, cocoa and banana plantations along the coastal plain, though the interior of the plateau is very sparsely inhabited.

Southern Brazil contains Porto Alegre (880 000) and is important for temperate crops, pigs and cattle, plus timber from the vast forests of pine.

Brazil occupies nearly half of South America.

Northern South America

Northern South America includes French Guiana, Surinam, Guyana, Venezuela, Colombia, Ecuador, Peru, Bolivia plus much of Brazil. It is entirely within the tropics.

It consists of the Amazon and Orinoco lowlands and narrow coastal plains. The Guiana Highlands occupy much of French Guiana, Surinam and Guyana, and also a large area in Venezuela. The Andes extend throughout this region. In Bolivia there are two ranges, with the Bolivian plateau in-between. There is also a Peruvian inter-montane plateau in between two Andean ranges, and another one in Ecuador. Colombia has three ranges, separated by the rivers Cauca and Magdalena, and the most easterly range extends into Venezuela beyond Caracas and reaching out towards Trinidad.

All these countries are poor and thinly populated, but do contain many mineral deposits. Venezuela has earned much foreign currency from oil, the main fields being located near Lake Maracaibo. There are rich iron mines in the Caroni Valley in south-east Venezuela. Guyana and Surinam are quite important for bauxite, and also have some gold and diamonds.

Group of Peruvian women and children showing the distinctive local dress.

Machu Picchu, a ruined Inca city, 3000 metres high in the Andes. It was discovered by Europeans in 1911.

Bolivia is particularly noted for tin, at Oruro and Uncia, though silver, lead, zinc and copper are also mined. The old silver mines of Bolivia attracted many Spaniards in the 16th and 17th centuries, when Potosi had over 150 000 inhabitants (present population = 60 000). Peru has many rich mineral deposits, notably at Cerro de Pasco (copper, lead, zinc), and Moquegua near Arequipa (copper).

The agriculture is mostly poor subsistence farming with maize and potatoes being the main food crops in the mountainous areas, with manioc in the tropical lowlands.

Llamas and sheep are reared on the Andean grasslands. There are a few areas of rich soil where commercial farming takes place. In the Andes of Colombia and Venezuela coffee is important, at 1000–2000 metres, and some cocoa is grown at lower altitudes. There are irrigated areas in the Peruvian Atacama where the rivers are supplied by water from melting snow in the Andes. Sugar cane and cotton are the main crops.

The capital cities – Caracas (2 184 000), Quito (597 000) and La Paz (605 000) are all situated high up in the Andes where climatic conditions are more favourable than in the hot, wet tropical lowlands. Lima, in Peru (3 158 000) is on the coastal lowlands in the Atacama desert.

Southern South America

Southern South America is mainly outside the tropics and includes the narrow part of the continent. Argentina, Uruguay, Chile, Paraguay and southern Brazil contain the temperate lands of South America. The Andes run parallel to the west coast, but between the mountains and the Pacific are stretches of desert in northern Chile, a Mediterranean type region in central Chile, and a mild wet forested area in southern Chile. East of the Andes are the grasslands of the Pampas, the Chaco scrub forest of Paraguay and northern Argentina, and semi-arid, poor grassland regions west and south of the Pampas. The grass-

The cowboys of the Pampas. Argentine gauchos shown breaking in a horse.

lands south of the Pampas are in the region of Patagonia.

Chile is a long, narrow country varying from completely dry uninhabited and uncultivable land in the north to very wet forested land in the south. Most people live in the middle third where there is sufficient rainfall to grow wheat, temperate and Mediterranean fruits including vines, and many subsistence food crops. Central Chile also contains many minerals, notably copper at Rancagua and coal near Concepcion. The presence of coal, which is uncommon in South America, has given rise to steelworks, and one of the few areas of concentrated industry in South America. Northern Chile is very dry, with Calama and Iquique averaging less than 2 mm per

186

Lakes and mountains, a typical scene of the southern Andes.

annum. The only settlements are associated with mining – mainly sodium nitrates and copper. Chuquicamata (28 000) is a large copper mining town situated 3000 metres up in the Andes. Southern Chile is also sparsely populated because it is too wet, receiving over 5000 mm in places.

The Chaco of Paraguay and northern Argentina is also sparsely populated, though it does provide some tannin and timber from quebracho trees, and a little cotton. South of the Chaco is the Pampas region, which is a vast expanse of temperate grassland covering more than half of Uruguay and much of Argentina between Buenos Aires and Bahia Blanca, and inland to the Andean foothills. Sheep and cattle are reared in large numbers, and wheat, maize and flax are grown. Large quantities of surplus food and wool are exported, mainly to Europe.

Buenos Aires (8 353 000) and Montevideo (1 376 000) are both capital cities located on the Pampas. They have many industries such as flour milling, meat freezing and canning, all dependent on the local agriculture. Asunción (388 000) is the capital of Paraguay, and Santiago (2 820 000) is capital of Chile.

All the large South American cities have impressive buildings and roads in the city centres, and often have skyscrapers. Around the edges of the cities are the shanty towns, built by poor people who have drifted from the countryside to the large towns in search of jobs.

187

Europe

Europe is a small continent, broken up into many countries, and containing many different languages. There are two separate languages spoken in Belgium, and three languages in Switzerland. Historical factors explain the large number of countries, as there have been many wars and numerous boundary changes, the last series of which came after the two world wars in 1918 and 1945.

As the continent is indented by the Mediterranean and Baltic Seas, nowhere in the continent is far from the sea. There are no large mountain ranges extending from north to south, and so climatic influences from the sea can spread across to the east.

Finland and parts of Russia consist of very old hard rock called the Baltic Shield, which has been worn down by millions of years of erosion. Northern Europe also contains many mountains, especially in Norway, Sweden and Scotland, which are very old – about 400 million years. South of these is the European plain which extends from Britain across Germany and Poland to Moscow. Southern Europe contains many faulted blocks, such as the Massif Central in France or the Meseta in Spain, which are also relics of old mountains which were formed about 250 million years ago.

There are also the young fold mountains which date from 40–50 million years ago and have not, therefore, been exposed to the forces of erosion for so long. These include the highest mountains in Europe such as the Alps, Pyrenees and Carpathians.

Some major cities and regional divisions of Europe.

Britain

The British Isles consists of Great Britain, Ireland, the Isle of Man, and adjacent islands, and make up one of the most densely populated areas in the world. England, Wales and Scotland together are called Great Britain, and with Northern Ireland make up the political unit of the United Kingdom. The Irish Republic is a completely independent country. Both the Irish Republic and the U.K. are part of the European Economic Community.

Name	Area (sq. km)	Population
Irish Republic (Eire)	70 000	3 086 000
England and Wales	151 000	49 195 000
Scotland	79 000	5 226 000
N. Ireland	14 000	1 547 000
Channel Islands	200	126 000
Isle of Man	590	56 000

The British Isles contain a rich variety of landscape, ranging from rugged hills in much of Scotland, North Wales, the Lake District and the mountains of Ireland, to the gentle undulations of southern England or central Ireland. The climate everywhere is mild and damp, except on the mountains where conditions are much more severe. There is much snow in winter and some patches last right through the summer in the Cairngorms.

There is intensive agriculture in the lowland areas, with market gardening, fruit and cereals. Dairying and sheep rearing are also successful. Pastoral farming is usually more important in the wetter west, and arable farming in the drier east.

Industries have grown up in many places, especially on the coalfields of South Wales and the north-east of England. Many new light industries are located in the south-east. The deposits of natural gas and oil which have been discovered in the North Sea will help to sustain British industries.

An English village and a rural landscape dominated by the church tower.

Scandinavia and Finland

Scandinavia consists of Norway, Sweden and Denmark, but Finland, Norway and Sweden are sometimes linked together as Fennoscandia.

Name	Area (sq. km)	Population
Denmark	43 000	5 045 000
Finland	337 000	4 682 000
Norway	324 000	3 987 000
Sweden	450 000	8 161 000
Iceland	103 000	215 000

Iceland is not really part of Scandinavia, but has had close links with Scandinavian countries in the past. It contains Europe's largest ice caps and there is much barren tundra. Most people live on the coast near Reykjavik, the capital (97 000) and Akureyri in the north. Sheep farming is the main activity on land, though tourists provide a useful source of income in summer. The geysers and hot springs are an interesting tourist attraction, but they also provide warm water for heating homes and greenhouses in Reykjavik.

Norway and Sweden contain many mountains, though eastern Sweden slopes gradually down to the Gulf of Bothnia. West Norway has a rugged coastline which is deeply indented by fjords such as Sogne fjord which extends nearly 200 kilometres inland. The only large lowland areas in Norway are near Trondheim and Oslo. Southern Sweden is a lowland region and is very similar to Denmark. Whereas most of Norway and Sweden have suffered from glacial erosion, both southern Sweden and Denmark have been covered by glacial deposits. Large areas would still be below sea level without these deposits.

Southern Sweden contains Lakes Vanern and Vattern which have formed in hollows in glacial

A view of Stockholm – sometimes called the Venice of the north.

deposits. Northern Sweden contains rock basin lakes in hollows scooped out by glaciers. Finland, which is the land of lakes, has some lakes in rock basin hollows eroded by ice sheets, and others are dammed by glacial deposits. The old hard rocks of Finland are part of the Baltic Shield which is now a low area because of erosion during the 3000 million years since the rocks first formed.

Western Norway and western Denmark have January temperatures just above zero but further east and north, winters are quite cold. July temperatures vary from 17°C in Denmark to less than 10°C in the far north of Sweden. Rainfalls are heavy, 2000–3000 mm in western Norway, but Finland receives only 500–600 mm. There is some tundra in the extreme north and on the mountains, and some deciduous forest in Denmark, but most of the land is naturally covered by coniferous forest.

Finland earns much income from forest products such as pulp and paper. Hydro-electric power is important in all three Fennoscandian countries. There is some farming in southern Finland, and dairying is particularly important. Hay, oats and potatoes grow well, and provide winter fodder for the animals, as well as food for the people. Much food has to be imported, though some butter and cheese is exported.

Sweden also exports dairy pro-

The Lapps are found in small numbers in the far north of Fennoscandia.

ducts and large quantities of forest products including matches. Near Kiruna in the Arctic there are large deposits of iron ore which are exported to Britain and Germany. There are also important industries such as shipbuilding, Volvo cars, ball bearings and washing machines, all of which are noted for their high quality.

Norway specialises in forest products and shipping, for which there has been a great tradition since the days of the Vikings. Denmark is most noted for high standards of agriculture, and is especially famous for butter, cheese and bacon. Co-operative farming is important and really well developed.

Western Europe

Western Europe contains the following countries:

Name	Area (sq. km)	Population
France	547 000	52 507 000
Belgium	31 000	9 804 000
Netherlands	34 000	13 541 000
Luxembourg	2 600	342 000
West Germany	249 000	62 041 000
Switzerland	41 000	6 481 000
Austria	84 000	7 528 000
East Germany	108 000	17 166 000

The northern part of this region is mostly low-lying, although there are a few faulted highland areas such as the Ardennes in Belgium or the Vosges in France. Further south is the Massif Central, beyond which Mediterranean conditions prevail. Southern Germany, together with Switzerland and Austria, contains the Alpine region with its steep hills and valleys.

Maritime influences make the climatic conditions quite mild, except in the mountains. Rainfall is normally adequate for agriculture, being 750–1000 mm in the west and 500–600 mm in the east. The natural vegetation, except in the Mediterranean part of France, was mostly deciduous forest, though much has now been cleared for agriculture.

France, Belgium, Netherlands, Luxembourg and West Germany are members of the European Economic Community. Austria and Switzerland are members of the European Free Trade Association, and East Germany belongs to the Warsaw Pact.

France contains many varied regions. The Paris Basin is a lowland area which is the most important economically. Rich soils are used for growing wheat, sugar beet and other crops, and there are many industries, especially in Paris (9 108 000), the capital. There is a coalfield in Nord near Valenciennes; this is the major industrial region in France, with steel, textiles, chemicals and many other indus-

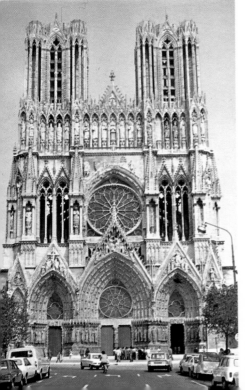

Reims cathedral, front view.

A view of the Inn valley in the Austrian Tyrol.

tries. Aquitaine is the second most productive lowland, growing wheat, maize, fruit and vines. The greatest wine area is Languedoc, though the best quality wine comes from near Dijon and in the Champagne area. The Alpine region is sparsely populated but is quite important as a source of hydro-electric power. Tourists attracted by the scenery in summer and skiing in winter are important to the economy of France, southern Germany, Switzerland and Austria.

Belgium, Netherlands and Luxembourg are three densely populated countries. There is rich farm-ing in the lowlands, including the polders, land reclaimed from the sea. Bulbs and cheese are specialities. There are also many industrial towns in the Belgian coalfield area, near Mons, and in the ports of Antwerp, Rotterdam and Amsterdam.

Both West and East Germany contain many industries, but the most important region is in the Ruhr. Here the rich coal deposits have provided the basis for steel, chemical and other industries. Iron is imported from Sweden and from Lorraine in France. Germany has been split into Eastern and Western parts, and Berlin (1 089 000) and Bonn (283 000), respectively, are the two capitals.

Eastern Europe

Eastern Europe consists of the following countries:

Name	Area (sq. km)	Population
Poland	313 000	33 691 000
Czechoslovakia	128 000	14 686 000
Hungary	93 000	10 458 000
Rumania	238 000	21 029 000
Bulgaria	111 000	8 679 000
Yugoslavia	256 000	21 153 000

This region is low-lying in the north, but is very rugged and mountainous in the south, where the Balkan Mountains of Bulgaria and the Dinaric Alps of Yugoslavia are located. To the north of these mountains are the low-lying Danube plain of Wallachia in Rumania and the plain of Hungary. Still further north are the Transylvanian Alps and the Carpathians, beyond which is the North European Plain.

Distance from the Atlantic gives continental climatic conditions with winter temperatures below zero and summer temperatures of 25°C. The natural vegetation changes from west to east because of the decreasing rainfall, and grasslands replace the forests, especially in the Plain of Hungary. The river Danube crosses the region, following its long and irregular route.

All the countries have been involved in warfare and boundary changes during the last 100 years, but now most national groups of people are located within one country. Since the Second World War these countries have been influenced by the U.S.S.R. and the

This colourful costume is from Lovetch in Bulgaria.

governments are Communist. The Communist rulers collectivised the farming, taking land away from the landowners and peasants and turning small farms into large collec-

194

tives. Several peasant families live and the work is planned by the manager of the collective. Large-scale farming methods and modern machinery are used.

Poland is low-lying in the north, but more rugged in the south. Warsaw (1 377 000) is the capital and is located on the river Vistula. The main ports are Gdansk (Danzig) and Szczecin (Stettin). There are rich deposits of coal and copper, and much coal is exported (36 million tons in 1973), including some to the U.K.

Czechoslovakia contains over 9 million Czechs and over 4 million Slovaks. The capital is Prague (1 091 000). There are rich deposits of coal, and oil is obtained from U.S.S.R. by pipeline.

Hungary consists of a great plain, surrounded by mountains. The plain is crossed by the Danube on which is located Budapest, the capital (2 039 000). Buda and Pest were twin towns on opposite sides of the river.

Rumania contains the Transylvania Alps and Carpathian Mountains, but also many lowlands, including the marshy delta region of the Danube. It has very varied scenery. The capital is Bucharest (1 529 000).

Bulgaria's capital is Sofia (946 000), which is located in-between the Rhodope and Balkan Mountains. The country is a mixture of picturesque mountains and broad plains leading down to the Black Sea.

Yugoslavia is mountainous in the south and west, but low-lying in the north where the Sava and Danube flow. Belgrade (1 204 000) is the capital. The Adriatic coast is Mediterranean in nature and attracts many tourists.

The rooftops in the old town of Prague, Czechoslovakia.

Mediterranean Europe

Mediterranean Europe contains the following countries:

Name	Area (sq. km)	Population
Portugal	92 000	8 735 000
Spain	505 000	35 225 000
Monaco	2	24 000
Italy	301 000	55 361 000
Albania	29 000	2 416 000
Greece	132 000	8 962 000
Malta	320	323 000

The Mediterranean area also takes in parts of France and Yugoslavia. Characteristic features are barren, rocky areas including some high mountains – for example, the Pyrenees or Apennines. There are also low-lying areas, many of which are extremely fertile.

Climatic conditions in the lowlands are very hot in summer (25°C) and mild in winter (5–10°C). Rain comes mainly in winter, leaving the summers scorching hot, dry and dusty. The vegetation has to be able to withstand the summer conditions, and to do this plants grow long roots to reach underground water, small leaves to reduce evaporation, waxy leaves or thick bark. The mountainous areas are normally wetter, and they often support coniferous trees with grassland at higher levels. This mountain grassland is known as Alpine pasture in all areas, not merely in the Alps.

Mediterranean Europe has been settled for many centuries and contains some of the most ancient areas of civilization in Greece and Italy. Standards are often quite low, however, and peasant farming is still common. Irrigation has been practised for centuries in many places, e.g. the slopes of Mount Etna, and

Cars racing round the streets of Monaco, with harbour beyond.

in Spain the irrigated regions are known as 'huertas'. The main crops include oranges, vines and olives, and intercropping is common.

Portugal faces the Atlantic and is therefore wetter than the other countries. Tourism is important, especially in the Algarve and the Azores and Madeira Islands. The Douro valley and Oporto are famous for port wine. Lisbon, the capital, (1 612 000) is on the river Tagus.

Spain consists of a high plateau, the Meseta, surrounded by coastal lowlands. Madrid (3 146 000) is the capital and has a very central location. Barcelona (1 745 000) is the main industrial town. Tourists are an important source of income, especially on the Mediterranean coast and the Balearic and the Canary Islands. The huertas grow many crops, including oranges, sugar cane, maize and vines. Seville is the centre of production for bitter oranges used to make marmalade. Jerez is a wine-producing area from which the name 'sherry' has been derived.

Southern France contains the small principality of Monaco, famous for Monte Carlo and the Grand Prix.

Italy is wealthy and industrialised in the north, especially in Milan, Turin and Genoa. There are also interesting towns such as Venice and Florence, which are famous for their beautiful old buildings and works of art. Rome (2 833 000) is the capital. Southern Italy, including

Gondola on a canal in Venice.

Sicily, tends to be very poor but conditions are improving, as more money is spent on roads, industry and irrigation schemes.

Greece is also quite poor, but attracts many tourists, who go there to enjoy the sunshine, the land and the archaeological beauty. Agriculture is important in certain areas, and grapes, tobacco and cotton are grown. The offshore islands are a great attraction.

Africa

North Africa

Country	Area (sq. km)	Population
Morocco	447 000	16 880 000
Algeria	2 382 000	16 275 000
Tunisia	164 000	5 641 000
Libya	1 760 000	2 240 000
Egypt	1 001 000	36 417 000
Mauritania	1 031 000	1 290 000
Mali	1 240 000	5 561 000
Niger	1 267 000	4 476 000
Chad	1 284 000	3 949 000
Western Sahara	266 000	108 000

Northern Africa includes the Sahara and all the lands to the north. Near the Mediterranean shores the climate is of the Mediter-

Major towns and regions of Africa.

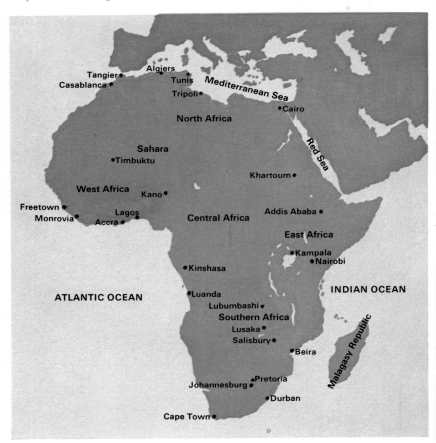

Trans-Sahara truck – lorries are used as buses in many parts of Africa.

ranean type with hot, dry summers and warm, wet winters. At Algiers the January average temperature is 10°C and in July it is 25°C. The total annual rainfall is 750 mm, most of which falls between October and March. At Timbuktu on the southern edge of the Sahara the corresponding three figures are 21°C, 34°C and 231 mm.

Northern Africa contains the Atlas Mountains in the north and the Hoggar and Tibesti ranges in the middle of the Sahara. Much of the Sahara is plateau with bare rock outcrops. There are also expanses of sand dunes, but these are smaller than the rock areas. The old trans-Saharan camel caravan routes and the modern motor routes follow the rocky areas.

Western Sahara, Mauritania, Mali, Niger and Chad are very sparsely populated. There are some groups of pastoralists living on the Saharan fringes, and crops are grown wherever water is available, as at Bamako in Mali or Niamey in Niger, both of which are on the river Niger. Ground nuts and cotton are the chief crops. There are some rich mineral deposits in these countries – for example, the iron mines of Fort Gouraud which are linked to Port Etienne by a railway.

Morocco, Algeria and Tunisia grow many crops, such as fruit and cereals near the coast, with dates inland. Phosphates are mined and there are rich oil and gas deposits in Algeria.

Libya is very sparsely populated but has a high income from oilwells in the interior. Egypt is densely populated along the Nile Valley, which is the greatest oasis in the world, watered by dams such as the Aswan. The Suez Canal is of great economic and political importance.

West Africa

Country	Area (sq. km)	Population
Senegal	196 000	4 315 000
Gambia	11 000	510 000
Guinea Bissau	36 000	517 000
Guinea	246 000	4 312 000
Sierra Leone	72 000	2 707 000
Liberia	111 000	1 669 000
Ivory Coast	322 000	4 765 000
Upper Volta	274 000	5 897 000
Ghana	239 000	9 607 000
Togo	56 000	2 171 000
Benin	113 000	3 029 000
Nigeria	924 000	61 270 000
Cameroon	475 000	6 282 000

Most of the West African countries were former colonies of Britain or France which have now gained independence. The coastal region is very wet and lush tropical rain forests grow there. Further inland, as the rainfall decreases, the forest becomes more open and then trees are gradually replaced by grassland. The grass becomes sparser as the grassland leads into the Sahara desert.

Lagos and Freetown both have temperatures above 25°C every month, and so growth is rapid, with heat and rain together. Near the coast, cocoa is the main cash crop, and palm oil is important. Yams are grown as food. Further inland, maize is the main food crop and cotton is grown for cash. On the drier grassland areas millet and ground nuts are grown, and many cattle and goats are reared. If there are too many of these animals they eat all

The costumes worn by some important tribal groups in West Africa.

Hausa
Yoruba
Yoruba
Hausa
Ibo

A Benin village with houses on stilts and waterways instead of paths.

the vegetation, and erosion of the soil occurs, causing the desert conditions to extend further south.

Nigeria is the largest country. It contains large reserves of oil in the Niger delta region, and there are tin and coal mines at Jos and Enugu, respectively. The coastal region is mangrove swamp. There are tropical forests inland which give way to savanna further north. Lagos (1 477 000) is the capital.

Cameroon contains both the Cameroon Peak which receives over 10 000 mm of rainfall per annum, and the semi-arid Lake Chad region in the north. The capital is Yaoundé (178 000).

Benin (formerly Dahomey) and Togo both grow oil palm products near the coast, with coffee and ground nuts being cultivated further inland. The capital of Togo is Lomé (193 000). Benin's capital is Porto Novo (85 000).

The most outstanding modern development in Ghana is the Volta scheme. When the river Volta was dammed at Akosombo, a large lake was formed and drowned many villages. Over 80 000 people had to be resettled in new towns. Cocoa is the most important crop and provides over half of the exports. Accra (738 000) is the capital.

The other West African States are sparsely populated but produce small crops for export, including cotton which is grown on the Ivory Coast. There are also mineral exports such as iron and diamonds from Sierra Leone, and phosphates from Senegal.

Liberia was created as a settlement for some freed American negroes in 1822. Monrovia (110 000) is the capital. Abidjan (510 000) is the capital of the Ivory Coast, and Dakar (581 000) is the capital of Senegal. Senegal's main export crop is ground nuts.

East Africa

Country	Area (sq. km)	Population
Sudan	2 506 000	17 324 000
Ethiopia	1 222 000	27 239 000
Somali Republic	638 000	3 090 000
Kenya	583 000	12 912 000
Uganda	236 000	11 172 000
Rwanda	26 000	4 123 000
Burundi	28 000	3 678 000
Tanzania	945 000	14 763 000
French Territory of Afars & Issas	22 000	104 000

This region contains the high mountains of Ethiopia and the vast plateau around Lake Victoria, with the Ruwenzori mountains on the western edge. Two branches of the great rift valley cross the plateau. Climate and vegetation vary throughout the region: there is hot, wet tropical forest on the Kenya and Tanzania coast, but desert in Somali and northern Sudan. Much of East Africa is a plateau covered by savanna, and is an elevated equatorial region similar to the lower parts of the tierra templada found in Andean countries. Many different tribal groups are found throughout East Africa.

Sudan is another country of extremes with Saharan conditions in the north and hot, wet forest in the south. The White and Blue Niles meet at Khartoum (648 000), the capital. Between the two Niles is the Gezira region with the Sennar dam, built in 1925, providing water for irrigation. Cotton is the major export, and gum-arabic is the next most important.

Ethiopia's capital is Addis Ababa (1 012 000) situated on a plateau at 2400 metres. Most people live in the upland area where climatic conditions are more favourable. Coffee is the leading cash crop and export. The eastern part of Ethiopia is very dry and similar to the Somali Republic. This is a sparsely populated country with many pastoral nomadic people. There are some small irrigated areas, but cattle, sheep, goats and camels are more important than crops. Mogadishu (230 000) is the capital.

Lions, with Mt Kilimanjaro, the highest peak in Africa, in the background.

Much of Kenya is plateau land on which animals are reared, but coffee, tea, pyrethrum and maize are important too. Coconuts are grown on the coastal lowlands. Mombasa (255 000) is the main port and Nairobi (535 000) is the capital. Kenya and Tanzania both attract many tourists with their wild animal life. Serengeti Plains are particularly famous but there are several game parks.

Tanzania now includes the islands of Zanzibar and Pemba which provide most of the world's cloves. Coconut, cotton, coffee and sisal are other important products. Animals of low quality are reared on the plateau. Gold, diamonds, lead and other minerals are being mined. Dar-es-Salaam (344 000) is the capital and chief port, and has railway links with Lake Tanganyika and also with Zambia.

Uganda grows cotton and coffee for export and has rich deposits of copper. The Owen Falls provide hydro-electricity. The capital is Kampala (331 000).

Rwanda and Burundi were formerly one Belgian colony but became two independent countries in 1962. Both countries contain parts of the rift valley and high mountains, including active volcanoes. Subsistence farming is the main activity, and financial aid is given by Belgium.

Kikuyu

Masai

Kamba

Masai

The costumes worn by some important tribal groups in East Africa.

Central Africa

Country	Area (sq. km)	Population
Central African Empire	623 000	1 716 000
Equatorial Guinea	28 000	305 000
Gabon	268 000	520 000
Congo	342 000	1 313 000
Zaire	2 345 000	24 222 000
Angola	1 247 000	5 798 000
Zambia	753 000	4 751 000
Malawi	118 000	4 900 000

Central Africa is mainly located in the basin of the river Zaire. This great lowland region is surrounded by high ground, the Adamawa mountains in the north, the Ruwenzori mountains or 'Mountains of the Moon' in the east, and the Bié Plateau in Angola. The central part of the basin is equatorial in character, with hot wet conditions every month. Dense forests grow near the

equator, but they thin out to open woodland in southern Zaire and northern Angola. All the countries are sparsely populated and underdeveloped, and have achieved independence from colonial powers quite recently. Explorers such as Stanley helped to open up this area during the 19th century.

Equatorial Guinea was once a Spanish colony. It grows cocoa, coffee and timber for export. Gabon, a former French colony, has similar products but also has rich deposits of iron ore.

The Central African Empire, formerly French, grows sorghum, ground nuts, coffee and cotton, as the climate is drier than in Gabon. Bangui (187 000) is the capital.

Congo was also formerly French and is located in the equatorial forest zone. Brazzaville (250 000) is the capital and is located on the river Zaire opposite Kinshasa

Stanley exploring the river Zaire

Pygmies are the original inhabitants of parts of the Central African forests.

(1 624 000) the capital city of Zaire. Zaire was formerly the Belgian Congo, and is potentially very wealthy. Palm oil, cocoa, coffee, rubber are exported, but the main source of income is from minerals. Copper, zinc, manganese and diamonds are exported, chiefly from Shaba Province in the south. Important railway lines run from Lubumbashi (357 000) the capital of Shaba, via Zambia to Dar-es-Salaam and Beira, or via Angola to Lobito.

Angola was formerly Portuguese and has been torn by warfare in recent years. Cattle, coffee and diamonds are important products. Luanda (475 000) is the capital.

Zambia, formerly British, is entirely inland and very dependent on rail links to Lobito and Dar-es-Salaam and Beira. There is much subsistence farming, but some tobacco is grown for export. The main source of income is minerals, especially copper, with some zinc, lead, cobalt and coal. The copper belt is around Kitwe and Mufulira, just across the border from Lubumbashi. Hydro-electric power is available from Kariba and elsewhere. The capital is Lusaka (348 000).

The capital of Malawi is Lilongwe (20 000), a new town, but Blantyre (169 000) is the main commercial centre. Most people are employed in agriculture and maize is the leading food crop.

Southern Africa

Southern Africa consists of extensive plateaux with mountains such as the Drakensbergs on the eastern rim.

Tropical grasslands of the north change to temperate grasslands as they go southwards. There are deserts on the west coast but forests are supported on the east coast by onshore winds from the Indian Ocean. There is a region of Mediterranean climate near Cape Town.

A Bantu (native) village in South Africa.

Rhodesia is mostly on the plateau. Maize is the main food crop, and cattle and tobacco both provide exports. Copper, asbestos, chrome and coal also earn much foreign currency. The Kariba scheme is important for hydro-electricity. The capital is Salisbury (502 000).

Mozambique was formerly Portuguese and is still mostly undeveloped. Some sugar, cotton and copra are exported, though most people are subsistence farmers. There are important railways to the interior. Beira and Maputo, the capital (355 000), are international ports.

Offshore is the large island of Madagascar, now known as the Malagasy Republic. The capital is Tananarive (378 000). Most people are subsistence farmers.

Botswana is very dry and sparsely populated. The main tribe is

A view of Cape Town showing wide streets and the docks in the background.

Bamangwato. The capital is Gaberone (18 000), and the chief exports are animal products.

South West Africa (Namibia) is even drier than Botswana, but does contain some diamond mines. Most people are pastoralists, and the main tribal groups are Ovambos, Hereros and Bushmen.

Lesotho is a small country surrounded by South Africa. Cattle, wool, mohair and diamonds are the main exports.

Swaziland is another small country which grows sugar, citrus fruits, maize and cotton. There are also deposits of iron, asbestos and wood.

The Republic of South Africa is noted for its apartheid policy, which segregates white people from all others. The others include Cape Coloureds who live near Cape Town, the Indians who are mainly in Natal, and the African negroes, or Bantu. There are many different tribes of Bantu, such as Zulu and Xhosa. South Africa is a very wealthy country with rich deposits of gold, diamonds and other minerals. The area around Cape Town is suitable for fruit-growing and cereals, and Natal grows much sugar cane. The interior plateau grows maize and a rich variety of crops wherever irrigation water from the Vaal or Orange rivers is available. Johannesburg, the largest town, grew up because of the local gold deposits.

U.S.S.R.

The European part of U.S.S.R. is correctly known as Russia, and is the most important part of the country. The U.S.S.R. consists of 15 republics, and the Russian Soviet Federal Socialist Republic (R.S.F.S.R.) is much the largest. R.S.F.S.R. is centred on Moscow and includes much of European Russia and the whole of Siberia.

The Republics of Russia are as follows (see also page 212):

Republic	Area (sq. km)	Population
R.S.F.S.R.	17 075 000	132 900 000
Ukraine	604 000	48 600 000
Belorussia	208 000	9 300 000
Georgia	70 000	4 900 000
Azerbaijan	87 000	5 500 000
Moldavia	34 000	3 800 000
Lithuania	65 000	3 300 000
Latvia	64 000	2 500 000
Armenia	30 000	2 700 000
Estonia	45 000	1 400 000

Winter temperatures are low throughout the entire region, only the Black Sea coasts being above zero in January. In July, the range is from over 20°C in the south to 10°C near the Arctic coast. Rainfall is low, falling from 750 mm in the wettest areas of the south-west, to only 250 mm in the north-east. The north is covered by tundra, south of which is a zone of coniferous forest extending to Leningrad. Moscow is in the mixed forest region and the extreme south is steppe land.

The tundra zone is sparsely populated, though the important port of Murmansk is located on the north coast. It is kept ice-free by the effects of the North Atlantic Drift.

The coniferous forest zone contains many lumber camps and sawmills. There are also wood pulp factories and many small settlements which practise dairy farming in clearings.

The mixed and deciduous forest

U.S.S.R. and neighbouring countries.

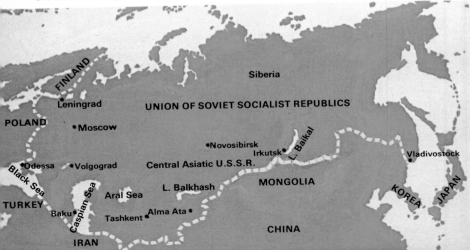

Red Square in Moscow, the scene of many impressive displays.

is well populated and contains many large cities such as Moscow (7 410 000), Gorki and Minsk. Moscow is the capital and in the centre of a big industrial area. Mixed farming is also practised.

The grassland region is not only important for growing crops such as wheat, maize, sugar beet and sunflowers, but also for industry. There are enormous deposits of coal near Donetsk, iron at Krivoy Rog and Kursk, and oil near Kuybyshev. There are many hydro-electric power schemes – notably along the river Volga which has now become a string of lakes as a result of all the dam construction. There are many large industrial towns in the Donetsk, Kharkov, Volgograd area.

To the east of the Black Sea are the Caucasus Mountains which contain the highest peaks in Europe. Beyond these mountains are the Transcaucasian republics of Georgia, Azerbaijan and Armenia. There are many fertile valleys in these republics, often with irrigation schemes, and Baku is an important oil producer.

Siberia

Siberia is U.S.S.R., east of the Ural Mountains and north of Central Asiatic U.S.S.R. It is governed from Moscow as part of the R.S.F.S.R. The total area is 13 402 000 sq. km and the population about 27 million.

This vast area is noted for its winter cold and more than half of Siberia is affected by permafrost. January average temperatures are minus 15°C in the south and minus 40°C in the north. The coldest places are Verkhoyansk and Oimyakon. July temperatures are 10°C in the north and 20°C in the south. Total rainfall varies from 375 mm to 200 mm, most of which falls in the summer. Winter is too cold for rain or even snow, and

Norilsk is a large and modern town in the Tundra regions of Siberia.

snowfalls are very light. Fierce blizzards with light drifting snow do occur occasionally. In spring the thaw causes very marshy conditions to develop. These are ideal for mosquitoes to breed in, and also make travel difficult.

Communications are difficult in Siberia because of the winter cold, and spring melt. Permafrost causes roads and railway lines to buckle because of expansion and contraction of water into ice, and back to water again. Distances are enormous, and there are very few people to make communications worthwhile. The enormous rivers Ob, Yenisey and Lena are used for navigation, especially transporting logs. They flow to the Arctic, unfortunately, which is away from likely markets, and they are frozen for up to 7 months each year. The southern sections of rivers melt first, but the

Bratsk Lake, Siberia, with logs felled in the local coniferous forests.

northern sections remain frozen until spring when extensive flooding can occur.

A few railway lines have been constructed and the longest is the Trans-Siberian Railway from Moscow to Vladivostok, a distance of 9300 kilometres. Moscow to Irkutsk (5470 kms) has been electrified. The South Siberian line links Magnitogorsk to Novokuznetsk, and the Turk Sib links Novosibirsk with Tashkent. Most of the towns are on these railways, and there is a thin ribbon of settlement stretching across Siberia.

There are vast areas of forests,

providing large quantities of logs and pulp. Many buildings are constructed of timber in the forested belt. There are also mineral deposits which encourage exploitation and settlement. Norilsk, north of the Arctic Circle, mines nickel, cobalt and copper, and sends them via a railway to Dudinka on the river Ob.

Novosibirsk (1 221 000) is the largest town and has many metallurgical industries. Novokuznetsk has large coal deposits and steel works. Yakutsk on the Lena is an important forestry town. Irkutsk on Lake Baykal is near a power station on the river Angara. Further down this river is the Bratsk hydroelectric station, one of the largest in the world.

Central Asiatic U.S.S.R.

Republic	Area (sq. km)	Population
Kazakhstan	2 717 000	13 900 000
Uzbekistan	447 000	13 300 000
Kirgizia	198 000	3 200 000
Tadzhikistan	143 000	3 300 000
Turkmenistan	488 000	2 400 000

Most of this region is south of 50° north, and Turkmenistan extends to 35° north. Therefore temperatures are higher than elsewhere in U.S.S.R. However, the location in the middle of the largest land masses causes winter temperatures to fall to an average of zero. Summer averages are very high, often over 30°C. The rainfall is less than 125 mm in many places, though in the north of Kazakhstan the annual total exceeds 250 mm and poor grassland or dry steppe can exist. Elsewhere, Middle Asia is a land of desert and high mountains, with a few densely populated oases such as the ancient settlements of Samarkand and Tashkent. The high mountains include the Pamirs which rise to 7495 metres in Communism Peak.

The populated parts of this region have been isolated from the remainder of U.S.S.R., but there are now four railway links which cross the deserts to the steppe lands further north. The Turk Sib extends from Alma Ata via the eastern end of Lake Balkash, the Trans Kazakhstan goes via Karaganda, the Kazalinsk line leads from Tashkent to Orenburg, and there is a line to the west of the Aral Sea.

There are many rich deposits of minerals which have encouraged the creation of industries. The Karaganda coalfield provides coal for the Ural industrial region, and also supports a local steel works. There is oil at Emba on the Caspian Sea and natural gas near Bukhara. Many swift rivers flow from the high mountains and these are being harnessed for hydro-electricity. Some of these rivers flow northwards into the desert and gradually dry up, but

Mechanised cotton picking in Turkmenistan.

Samarkand. Ruins of the Bibi Khanum mosque.

do provide water for irrigation.

In Turkmenistan some of the largest irrigated areas are near Ashkhabad (272 000). There is local water but also Amu Darya water transported 800 km by the Kara Kum canal. Cotton and wheat are the main crops.

The Amu Darya also supports agriculture near Khiva, and in the mountainous area in the south. Cotton is again the main crop, but cereals, fodder crops and fruits are also grown.

The Syr Darya is another important source of irrigation, especially in the Fergana Basin. One quarter of the U.S.S.R. cotton crop is grown here, together with apricots, mulberries for silkworms and vines. Tashkent (1 504 000) is an oasis town with important cotton industries; it is the capital of Uzbekistan. Frunze (463 000), capital of Kirgizia, is another oasis town, but cereals and sugar beet are the specialities.

There are many areas used for stock raising, with sheep, goats and camels. Many mountain pastures are utilised in summer.

Tashkent is an ancient town and was a focus of caravan routes across the desert over 1000 years ago. Samarkand is a much older oasis, dating from 3000 B.C. or earlier. It is now an industrial city.

213

Asia

Middle East

Country	Area (sq. km)	Population
Turkey	781 000	38 270 000
Syria	185 000	7 121 000
Lebanon	10 000	2 784 000
Israel	21 000	3 299 000
Jordan	98 000	2 618 000
Iraq	435 000	10 765 000
Iran	1 648 000	31 955 000
Saudi Arabia	2 150 000	8 706 000
Yemen	195 000	6 477 000
South Yemen	288 000	1 633 000
Oman	212 000	743 000
United Arab Emirates	84 000	215 000
Qatar	11 000	89 000
Kuwait	18 000	929 000
Bahrein	620	243 000

This region contains many high mountain ranges and extensive plateaux, especially in Yemen, Turkey and Iran. In spite of this, the entire area is very dry, mostly receiving less than 500 mm. The only wetter areas are the Yemeni Mountains and the Mediterranean coastlands. Summer temperatures are high, over 25°C everywhere, and winters range from 5°C in Turkey to over 20°C in Southern Arabia.

Much of the Middle East is desert, sparsely populated and barren. There are some successful agricultural regions near the Mediterranean coasts and in areas of irrigation. Turkey grows vines, fruit, cotton, tobacco and cereals, and Lebanon and Syria also have some rich farming areas. Israel produces many fruits, including Jaffa oranges, and contains many highly successful irrigation schemes in former desert lands.

The largest expanses of irrigation are in the area historically known as Mesopotamia, the land between the rivers Tigris and Euphrates. This is a focal point of early civilization and

Major towns of Asia.

has been farmed for thousands of years. The main towns are Baghdad, the capital of Iraq, (2 969 000), Basra (371 000) and Mosul (293 000). Rice is the main summer crop and wheat the winter. Eighty per cent of the world's trade in dates comes from Iraq. Oil is the greatest export, however, mainly coming from the Kirkuk area. There are pipelines to take this oil to the Mediterranean.

Many other countries earn most of their foreign currency from oil – for example, Iran, Saudi Arabia, Kuwait, Bahrein and the United Arab Emirates. Many of these countries will be quite poor without oil, and must use their revenues of oil sales to develop industries and provide amenities for the future. Iran is different from most of the large oil producers in having many other sources of wealth. The capital is Tehran (3 858 000) which is an important industrial town. Wheat, rice and cotton are the main agricultural products and much wool is produced. Esfahan (575 000), the second biggest town, is the centre of carpet making.

Saudi Arabia is a large sparsely populated country whose major oil fields are near Abquiq. The capital, Riyadh (300 000), is located well inland and another important town is Mecca (250 000), the focal point of the Moslem religion.

Colourful national costumes from the Middle East.

Typical Arab dress

Dubai

Bedouin

Indian Sub-Continent

Country	Area (sq. km)	Population
Afghanistan	647 000	18 796 000
Pakistan	888 000	68 214 000
Nepal	141 000	12 319 000
Bhutan	47 000	1 146 000
Bangladesh	144 000	74 991 000
India	3 288 000	586 266 000
Sri Lanka	66 000	13 679 000

This region is very mountainous in the north, with the Himalayas and other ranges such as the Karakoram and Hindu Kush. There are also mountains, such as the Western Ghats in Peninsula India, and even the mountains of Sri

This old fashioned method of winnowing rice is still used in India.

Lanka rise to 2524 metres in Pidurutalagala.

There are many climatic variations caused by relief. The lowlands average 10°C in the north in January and 20°C in the south, whereas in July the temperatures are over 25°C everywhere, but often exceed 30°C in inland areas. The rainfall exceeds 2500 mm on the Western Ghats and Himalayan foothills, but falls as low as 200 mm in parts of the Thar Desert of India.

Afghanistan is a sparsely populated mountainous country, but is self-sufficient in food. Wool and karakuls (Persian lamb skins) are exported.

Pakistan is also mountainous in

the north and west, but there are lowlands too. These are too dry for much settlement, and all the agriculture is dependent on the river Indus. Dams and irrigation canals are essential. Some of the Indus comes across from India, and the two countries have peaceful agreements to regulate the use of the water. Islamabad (77 000) is the new capital, but Karachi (3 409 000) is the main town and port.

Nepal is a Himalayan State still governed by a king. The capital is Katmandu (210 000). Bhutan is another Himalayan country which is influenced and aided by India. The capital is Thimphu.

Bangladesh was formerly East Pakistan but became independent in 1971. It consists mainly of the delta lands of the rivers Ganges and Brahmaputra and is low-lying and very wet in summer, when the monsoon floods arrive. Seventy-five per cent of the people work on the land, and 90% of the farmed land is used for rice. Jute is the most important cash crop, and half the world's supplies are grown here. Dacca (1 310 976) is the capital.

India is a large and well populated country, and consists of 21 states. Seventy per cent of the people work on the land and grow rice, wheat, millet, sugar cane and cotton in suitable regions. There are many irrigation schemes ranging from highly efficient dams and canals to the primitive tanks. These are

Benares, the sacred Hindu city, is on the banks of the Ganges.

merely embanked fields that can trap flood water. India has rich mineral deposits such as coal, oil, gas, manganese and iron, and there are many industrial developments – for example, Bombay, Calcutta and Jamshedpur. The capital is Delhi (3 029 000).

Sri Lanka was formerly called Ceylon and has a hot and wet tropical climate. Rice and coconuts are grown on the lowlands, and tea and rubber are grown on the slopes of the mountains where rainfall is high, but drainage is good. Colombo (562 160) is the capital.

China and Neighbours

Country	Area (sq. km)	Population
China	9 561 000	824 961 000
Mongolia	1 565 000	1 403 000
South Korea	99 000	33 459 000
North Korea	121 000	15 439 000
Taiwan	36 000	15 000 000

China and the adjacent countries contain a varied mixture of high mountains such as Everest and the Himalayas, a high plateau in Tibet and flat lowlands as in the Yangtse valleys. There are hot wet areas in Southern China, and very cold and dry areas in Sinkiang. There are densely populated regions in the south and east, but lands so empty in the west that space for a nuclear weapon-testing ground was available, and people did not have to be moved from their homes.

Taiwan is an offshore island which used to be known as Formosa. Exiles from China settled here when the Communists took over China in 1949. Rice, bananas, sugar cane, pineapples and many other crops are grown. Coal, gold and sulphur are mined, and there are growing industries, including ship-building.

Korea was formerly one country, but was divided into two by the 38th parallel of latitude, and a war was fought over this boundary in 1950–51. Pyongyang (1 500 000) is capital of North Korea, and Seoul (5 536 000) is capital of South Korea. South Korea grows much rice, barley, wheat and tobacco and has rich tungsten mines. North Korea has many mineral deposits, notably coal, iron, lead, zinc and copper, but agriculture is not well developed. However, the farms have been collectivized, machinery has been provided by China and U.S.S.R., and there are now several irrigation schemes. Both Koreas are developing industries in the major towns.

The Mongolian People's Republic was a province of China until 1911, but is now independent. It is sparsely populated and most people are pastoralists, rearing horses, camels, cattle, sheep and goats. There are some mineral deposits

Pole junk from . oochow in China

which have not yet been exploited. Ulan Bator (282 000) is the capital.

China contains nearly one quarter of the world's people and has many large towns. Shanghai has over 7 million inhabitants, Peking over 5 million, Tientsin 3 600 000, Shenyang 2 800 000, Wuhan 2 560 000, Canton 2 500 000 and there are 15 other cities with over 1 million. It is a mountainous country crossed by the rivers Hwang, Yangtse and Si. The main lowlands are in the Si Kiang valley (*kiang = river*) and on the great northern plain extending from the Yangtse to the Hwang. The climatic conditions change from hot and wet in the south-east to very cold and dry in the north-west.

There are very high population densities, up to 800 per square kilometre in the rich farming lands of the Si and Yangtse deltas. Floods deposit silt to restore fertility each year, and two or three crops of rice can be grown. Tea is also important in southern China, on the terraced hillsides. Wheat is the main food crop in northern China, and cotton is grown. Millet and kaoliang are the staple food crops in the driest and coldest lands. There is much industrial development too, especially in Manchuria at Anshan, Fushun and Shenyang, using local coal and iron deposits. Minerals have also given rise to industries in Wuhan and Chungking in the Yangtse valley. Shanghai is an important port and industrial centre.

The rare panda is one of the world's best loved animals.

Japan and the Philippines

Both of these countries consist of a collection of islands, but whereas the Philippines are between 5 and 20°N, Japanese islands extend from 31 to 45°N, with obvious climatic differences.

The Philippines consist of over 7000 islands, though 11 account for 95% of the total area. Luzon (113 000 sq. km) and Mindanao (198 000 sq. km) are the largest. There are many high mountains, active volcanoes, small lowland areas and plains. Luzon has two large plains and Mindanao has one. Temperatures are always high – over 25°C – and rainfall is heavy. The west coasts are wet from June to December, when the south-west monsoon blows, and dry during the rest of the year while the north-east trades blow. The east coasts receive rain throughout the year as there are also south-east monsoon winds in summer. A few areas have less than 1000 mm per annum but mostly the total is over 2000 mm.

The population is very mixed, consisting of natives, Malays, Chinese and Spaniards. There are some very densely populated areas surrounded by empty, mountainous regions. Over half of the people are farmers, though only one sixth of the land is cultivated. Rice, maize and yams are the main food crops, and there are plantation crops too. These include coconut, sugar cane, bananas and manila hemp fibre. Coconut products (copra and oil) are the main exports, and sugar and hemp are next in importance. Most trade is with the U.S.A. There are

Costumes from Hokkaido, the most northerly of the Japanese islands.

several mineral deposits, notably copper, and there is a growing number of small industries. Manila (1 436 000) is the largest town, but Quezon City (896 000) has become the capital. The Republic of the Philippines has been in existence since 1946.

Japan consists of four main islands – Hokkaido, Honshu, Kyushu and Shikoku. They are all mountainous and volcanic with areas of coastal lowlands. The major lowlands are the Kwanto Plain near Tokyo, the Nobi Plain near Nagoya, and the Kinki or Osaka Plain. The climate in monsoonal, though the winter winds from Asia do bring rain to the west coast. The warm Kuro Siwo current washes both sides of Japan though the cold Kurile current affects Hokkaido and northern Honshu occasionally in summer. Typhoons

occur most summers.

Less than 20% of the workers are engaged in farming, a much lower figure than in most of Asia. Farming is intensive and yields are high. Two or three crops are often grown together, and mountain-sides are terraced to increase the size of the crops. Rice is the main foodstuff and two crops a year are grown in the south-east. Wheat, barley, fruits, tea and mulberries (for silk worms) are important.

Agriculture is very productive and so, too, are the fisheries and industry. Japan is the world's number one fishing nation, and has a wide range of industrial products such as ships, cars, textiles, radios and cameras. Tokyo (11 582 000) is the capital, and with the neighbouring towns of Yokohama and Kawasaki is the major industrial area of Japan – it is, in fact, one of the greatest in the world. The Osaka (2 889 000)–Kobe (1 325 000) area is another big industrial region.

Rice paddy terraces on a hillside in the Philippines.

South-East Asian Mainland

Country	Area (sq. km)	Population
Socialist Republic of Vietnam	333 000	43 198 000
Laos	237 000	3 257 000
Kampuchea	181 000	7 888 000
Thailand	514 000	41 023 000
Burma	678 000	30 310 000
Malaysia	330 000	11 700 000
Singapore	580	2 219 000

South-East Asia contains many mountain ranges such as the Arakan Yoma in Burma, and large rivers such as the Irrawaddy and Mekong. The climate is monsoonal. Winds are mainly south-westerly in summer and north-easterly in winter. Thus, eastern coasts such as Vietnam receive most rain in winter, whereas the west coasts are wettest in summer. Rainfall is usually high, over 1500 mm, and temperatures are over 20°C. The heat and moisture combine to promote rapid growth in the wet season and vegetation is dense; jungle is widespread. The monsoon forests contain teak, ironwood (pynkado), banyan, sandalwood and bamboo.

Traditional costumes from Burma.

The areas with lower rainfall tend to have open woodland with patches of tropical grass.

Population densities vary a lot from Singapore to Laos, but in most countries there are heavily populated areas where rich soils occur, and there are empty areas in the mountains and forests. Most of the people are quite poor, and often hungry.

In 1975 with the collapse of the Thieu regime in South Vietnam, North and South Vietnam were reunified as the Socialist Republic of Vietnam. The country consists of two large delta lowlands on the Red River (in the north) and on the Mekong River (in the south), linked by a long mountainous backbone. The country's tropical monsoon climate favours rice growing, especially in the Mekong delta. Other crops are rubber, tea and coffee. Minerals (coal, tin, chrome, phosphates) are restricted to the north. The Vietnamese, who comprise more than 80 per cent of the population, are a Mongolian race of Chinese culture, Buddhist religion

Elephants carrying a log in the Burmese forest.

and Indo-Chinese language, using the Latin alphabet. Before World War II, Vietnam was divided into three French colonial areas.

Kampuchea was formerly known as Cambodia and is bordered by Thailand, Laos and Southern Vietnam. It contains Lake Tonlé Sap which is surrounded by a large lowland basin. The lake drains to the Mekong in winter, but in summer Mekong flood water flows into the lake which grows to 10 000 sq. kilometres, four times its winter size. Agriculture and fishing are the two chief activities. Phnom-Penh (2 000 000) is the capital.

Thailand and Burma both contain rich rice-growing areas in the Irrawaddy and Menam deltas, and surpluses are exported. Burma has some minerals, notably oil, and both countries export teak. Ran-goon (3 187 000) is the capital of Burma and Bangkok (1 867 000) of Thailand.

The Federation of Malaysia consists of Malaya, Sarawak and Sabah in Borneo. Formerly a member of the Federation, Singapore seceded in 1965 to become an entirely independent State. The west coastal lowlands of the Malay Peninsula have been cleared of much dense tropical jungle and the land is used to grow rice and cash crops; the east coast has some cultivated land. Rice, palm oil, coconuts and pineapples are important. There are rich deposits of tin, and also some iron and bauxite. Kuala Lumpur (452 000) is the capital.

Singapore is a group of islands forming an independent State off the southern tip of the Malay Peninsula. The city of Singapore is one of the world's largest transit ports, and one of the great commercial centres of South-East Asia.

Indonesia

Indonesia comprises Sumatra, Java, Kalimantan or Borneo, Sulawesi, Irian or New Guinea, and many smaller islands. The non-Indonesian areas in the old East Indies are as follows: Sarawak, Brunei and Sabah in Borneo, Portuguese Timor and Papua New Guinea.

Sabah and Sarawak are part of Malaysia. Sabah covers 80 000 sq. km and has a population of 650 000 of whom 420 000 are natives and most of the remainder Chinese. Most people are subsistence farmers but there are some rubber plantations. The main exports are timber and tannin from the forests. The interior is forested and mountainous, rising to over 4000 metres in Mt Kinabalu.

Sarawak has an area of 121 000 sq. km and 975 000 inhabitants including 380 000 Dyaks, 290 000 Chinese and 180 000 Malays. Rubber, logs, sago and pepper are the main exports.

Brunei has an area of 5800 sq. km and a population of 144 000. It became an independent country in 1963. The main wealth is oil, which accounts for over 90% of the exports.

Papua New Guinea is the eastern half of New Guinea, having an area of 462 000 sq. km and a population of 2 652 000. Coconuts, cocoa, coffee, rubber, sago and oil palms are grown, and copper is mined. Most of the country is undeveloped at present. Its fauna resembles that of Australia.

The Portuguese part of Timor covers 15 000 sq. km and has a population of 658 000.

Indonesia became independent in 1945. It covers 1 904 000 sq. km and has a population of 128 509 000. 80 million live on Java, 21 million on Sumatra, 9 million on Sulawesi and 6 million on Kalimantan. Most of the people are Moslems. The main crops grown are rice, maize, sugar cane, tea, coffee and rubber. Tin, bauxite and coal are mined but oil is the most important mineral, accounting for more than one-quarter of the total exports.

The islands of Indonesia are spread out over 12 million square kilometres. They are mountainous and highly volcanic. Many rich farming areas have resulted from ancient volcanic outbursts, but there have been disasters too, notably at Krakatoa, situated between Sumatra and Java. The climate is equatorial with some monsoonal influences. Temperatures are about 25°C every month, and the rainfall ranges from 1500 to 3500 mm per annum. Dense forest is widespread, though much has been cleared in Java, Madura and Bali.

Java is the most important island and contains Djakarta (4 576 000) – the capital of Indonesia, Surabaya (1 556 000) and Bandung (1 202 000). Java was helped in its early development by the Dutch. It has a very fertile soil, and mountain

Java

Javanese dancer

Bali

Traditional costumes
from different
Indonesian islands

Sumatra

slopes have been terraced. Peasant
farmers have smallholdings and
there are also large plantations.

Sumatra is larger than Java and is
potentially very rich. Agriculture
could be extended and there are
deposits of oil, coal and many other
minerals. Medan (636 000) is the
main town. Banka and Billiton, off
the coast of Sumatra, are granite
islands with rich tin deposits.

Kalimantan is the Indonesian
share of Borneo. It is mountainous
and forested, and largely undeveloped. Most of the people are subsistence farmers in Kalimantan and
also in Sulawesi, which is the fourth
largest island of Indonesia.

225

Australia

State or Territory	Area (sq. km)	Population
Capital Territory	2 400	180 000
New South Wales	801 000	4 754 000
Northern Territory	1 347 000	702 000
Queensland	1 728 000	1 969 000
South Australia	984 000	1 216 000
Tasmania	68 000	399 000
Victoria	228 000	3 627 000
Western Australia	2 527 000	1 191 000

The six states of Australia have their own governments and the two territories are controlled directly by the central Parliament in Canberra. Australia is a vast island continent with a plateau occupying over 2 million square kilometres in the west, and the Great Dividing Ranges creating a formidable barrier in the east.

Climate and vegetation are very varied because of the great size of Australia. The horse latitudes high pressure belt causes the dry conditions over much of western and central Australia. In summer the rainy monsoon winds affect the north and support forests along the coast, with grass inland. The east coast is also wet because of winds from the sea and forests extend from Queensland to Tasmania. On the western side of the Great Divide, the rainfall is able to support grassland, but there is nothing but desert further inland. Westerly winds affect the southern parts of Australia. They blow over Tasmania throughout the year, and a maritime climate supports forest growth. These winds move further north in winter (July) and bring rain to the Adelaide and Perth regions, both of which have a Mediterranean climate.

Before the arrival of the European, the only inhabitants were the Aborigines who reached Australia

Australia and the neighbouring seas.

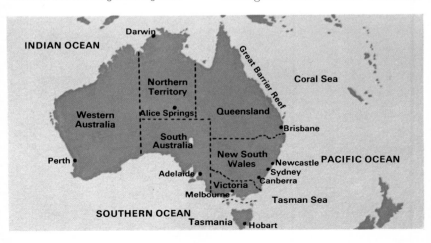

A view of Canberra showing the planned avenues and mountains nearby.

several thousand years ago. Australia's isolation from other land masses has also had a considerable effect on the animal life. Such unusual marsupials as the kangaroo and koala bear, and monotremes (egg-laying mammals) like the duck-billed platypus are unique to Australia.

Australia is a wealthy country in terms of resources, in spite of the vast expanse of desert which is never likely to have many inhabitants.

Agriculture is mainly practised in the south-east, on the east coast, and in the south-west corner which is where most of the people live, and where rainfall is most reliable. The country has widespread reserves of iron, coal, copper, gold, lead, zinc and other minerals. Much iron is being extracted from the hottest and driest part of Australia in the Hamersley area of Western Australia. New railway lines have been built to serve these iron mines, and there are other important railway lines such as the trans-continental from Perth to Adelaide, Sydney and Melbourne. Because of the great distances involved, air travel is very important in

The platypus has a duck's bill, webbed feet and lays eggs.

227

An Australian farmer driving his sheep back to the farm for dipping.

Australia, and there is a Flying Doctor service to isolated settlements.

The only well populated area of Western Australia is the south west corner near Perth, the capital (739 000), which contains over 60% of the total inhabitants. Fruits and cereals are grown near the coast, and wheat and sheep farming are important inland, though much of the interior is empty desert. Kalgoorlie on the main transcontinental railway grew up as a gold mining town, and still has water piped from a reservoir near Perth. The northern part of the State contains the rich iron mines, some irrigated land in the Ord valley, and grazing territory in the Kimberley area.

The Northern Territory is very sparsely populated. Pastoral farming for beef is the main activity, but minerals such as manganese from Groote Eylandt, and gold and copper from Tennants Creek earn more money. A railway runs from Darwin, the chief town, inland to Birdum, and a road continues southwards to Alice Springs and the South Australian railway.

The capital of South Australia is Adelaide with 868 000 people. In this area, fruits, vines and cereals are grown, and there are sheep further inland. The iron mines on the Eyre Peninsula provide ore which is sent via Whyalla to steel works in New South Wales.

Queensland contains the Great Artesian Basin, the world's greatest source of artesian water. This helps to support pastoral farming in the interior. The wetter coastlands have sugar plantations and grow tropical fruits. Offshore is the Great Barrier Reef. There are several important mining centres, such as Mt Isa, for copper, silver, lead and zinc, Mt Morgan for copper and gold, and Weipa for bauxite. There are oil and gas deposits inland from Brisbane (911 000) which is the state capital.

New South Wales is the most populated state, and contains Sydney (2 874 000), the largest city of Australia. The wet coastal plain produces milk, vegetables, cereals and fruit, and inland there is also important farming. Wheat and sheep farms are located on the western slopes of the Dividing Ranges, and sheep are reared further inland

too. There are over 50 million sheep in New South Wales. There are irrigated areas along the Murrumbidgee and Murray rivers, and these have been extended by water from the Snowy River scheme. This scheme has diverted water which used to flow to the Tasman Sea. There is an important coalfield near Newcastle and lead, silver and zinc mines at Broken Hill.

Victoria contains Melbourne (2 584 000), the second city of Australia, and also some rich farming including irrigated tracts in the Murray Darling Basin. The Murray Darling grassland area is the most productive part of Australia.

Tasmania is the smallest, and wettest state, and is noted for its forest and temperate crops such as potatoes. There are hydro-electric power schemes supported by the heavy rainfall. Hobart (158 000) is the capital.

A view of Alice Springs showing the main street.

New Zealand

New Zealand has a population just over 3 000 000, of whom 290 000 live in Auckland, 285 000 in Christchurch, 140 000 in Wellington, and 112 000 in Dunedin. There are 230 000 Maoris and most of these live in the North Island, especially near Auckland and Rotorua. The North Island contains 2 200 000 people in 114 000 sq. km, and South Island has 842 000 in 153 000 sq. km.

North Island consists of a mountain core which contains active volcanoes and geysers. This is surrounded by lowlands, notably the Auckland–Hamilton area and the Taranaki lowlands which surround Mt Egmont, an extinct volcano.

Major towns of New Zealand.

South Island has a mountainous west, where the Southern Alps reach 3764 metres in Mt Cook and contain many glaciers. The east is lower, especially on the Canterbury Plains. The climate is warm in the north, where Auckland averages 11°C in the coldest month and 20°C in the hottest, with 1200 mm of rain spread throughout the year. Dunedin in the south has figures of 7°C, 15°C and 930 mm.

The climate is always suitable for the growth of grass and so pastoral farming is very important. There are over 55 million sheep and 10 million cattle. Butter, cheese, beef, wool and lamb are important exports. Other exports include hides and skins, apples, vegetables, newsprint and pulp.

New Zealand was first settled by the Moriori, who are now extinct, and then by the Maoris who came by canoe from islands in Polynesia. They lived mainly in North Island which was one of the reasons why the earliest British settlers from 1840 onwards went to South Island. Gradually, the North Island has overtaken South Island's population because conditions for rearing cattle are more suitable in the north. Most of the agricultural produce was sold in Europe, especially Britain, in exchange for manufactured goods, but the E.E.C. has encouraged New Zealand to look for new markets such as Japan.

New Zealand is a very sparsely populated country and could sup-

Maori traditional costumes are still worn on ceremonial occasions.

port many more people. The two islands contain a wealth of beautiful scenery, and also large expanses of good agricultural land. There are rich forests and small deposits of gold and coal. Oil has been discovered, and the heavy rainfall and high mountains provide hydro-electric power schemes such as in the Waikato and Waitaki rivers. There is also some geothermal power produced.

The Southern Alps have dramatic scenery and attract many tourists.

Oceanic Islands

There are hundreds of oceanic islands, many of which are very isolated. They are mainly the tips of volcanoes which have grown up from the sea bed, or they consist of coral. Some are uninhabited, but those with people often show similar human characteristics. For example, the island folk are often expert boatmen and include fishing as one of their main activities. They are independent and versatile people because their isolation has made it necessary for them to do all their own jobs.

The Atlantic contains many famous islands such as the Canaries, Iceland, Tristan da Cunha, and the Azores. The Indian Ocean contains Madagascar, Mauritius, and the Seychelles. The Pacific Ocean contains the Hawaiian Islands, Fiji, Easter Island, Galapagos, Christmas Island and Juan Fernandes.

Iceland is highly volcanic, as are many smaller Atlantic islands. Tristan da Cunha islands are situated at 37° south. The main island consists of a volcano rising to 2060 metres. It erupted in 1961 and all the inhabitants were evacuated to Britain, but many returned in 1963. They grow potatoes and some fruit, rear animals and catch fish.

The Azores and Cape Verde are Portuguese islands and are also volcanic in origin. They attract tourists and grow vegetables and fruit for export.

The Canary Islands are Spanish and they export many potatoes and tomatoes to Britain. Their sunny climate also attracts many tourists, especially in winter. They provide ports of call for many cruise liners and have been important to trans-Atlantic sailing, as many early explorers such as Columbus set sail from the Canaries.

In the Indian Ocean, Mauritius and the Seychelles are amongst

Caroline Islands in Micronesia. A feast of turtle meat.

A group of iguanas on Narborough Island, Galapagos.

the well-known small islands. Mauritius became independent in 1968. It covers 1800 sq. km and has a population of 830 000. The main crop and export is sugar cane. Other crops are tea, tobacco and potatoes.

The Seychelles contain 86 islands which cover 277 sq. km. The capital is Victoria, on the main island Mahé. Coconuts, vanilla and tea are grown. The people also depend on fishing and a growing tourist industry for their livelihood. The construction of a runway here – as in so many islands – has enabled package tour flights to land with loads of tourists.

The Pacific contains thousands of islands, many of which are coral islands with palm trees. The small islands of Polynesia and Micronesia are often coral, and there are many atolls.

The Hawaiian Islands are volcanic. They make up the 50th state of the U.S.A. The Galapagos are also volcanic. They belong to Ecuador and cover an area of 7800 sq. km. There are seven principal islands. It is interesting that on each island there are finches which are slightly different from those of the other islands. It was these differences that encouraged Darwin to write about evolution, as he believed that each type of finch had evolved to suit the environment of the island on which it was living.

Easter Island belongs to Chile, and is famous for its enormous carved stone figures, 9–12 metres tall and weighing up to 8 tonnes. The island is volcanic and is peopled by Polynesians, who grow tobacco, sugar cane and root crops.

The Juan Fernandez Islands off the coast of Chile contain the Mas a Tierra. This was the island on which Alexander Selkirk was put ashore and abandoned for 4 years and 4 months in 1704. The captain of the ship that rescued him wrote an account of the episode. It was on this account that the story of Robinson Crusoe was based.

Index